FIRE

FROM

HEAVEN

'When Solomon had finished praying,
fire came down from heaven and consumed
the burnt offering and the sacrifices;
and the glory of the Lᴏʀᴅ filled the temple.

'And the priests could not enter the house
of the Lᴏʀᴅ, because the glory of the Lᴏʀᴅ
had filled the Lᴏʀᴅ's house.

'When all the children of Israel saw how the fire
came down, and the glory of the Lᴏʀᴅ
on the temple, they bowed their faces to the
ground on the pavement, and worshipped
and praised the Lᴏʀᴅ, saying:

"For He is good,
for His mercy endures for ever"'

(2 Chronicles 7:1-3).

FIRE

FROM

HEAVEN

TIMES OF EXTRAORDINARY REVIVAL

Paul E. G. Cook

PUBLISHING WITH A MISSION

EP BOOKS
Faverdale North, Darlington, DL3 0PH, England

www.epbooks.org

e-mail: sales@epbooks.org

EP BOOKS USA
P. O. Box 614, Carlisle, PA 17013, USA

www.epbooks.us

e-mail: usasales@epbooks.org

First published 2009

British Library Cataloguing in Publication Data available

ISBN 13   978-085234-709-6   ISBN 0-85234-709-X

Printed and bound in Great Britain by the MPG Books Group

CONTENTS

LIST OF ILLUSTRATIONS

PREFACE

This work has a history. Since giving a paper on *The Forgotten Revival* at the Westminster Conference in 1984, and subsequently a number of addresses in various places on different aspects of that revival movement, friends have urged me to write up the material in book form to ensure a more permanent record of these revivals. My calling as a preacher has kept me from doing this. However, further exhortations have finally prevailed and this book is the result, with occasional evidences of the preacher still present.

The 'Methodism' which forms a significant part in my account has little or no similarity to the modern version of that name. The Methodists of the eighteenth century were the product of the Evangelical Revival, and those who followed in the early decades of the nineteenth century were wedded to the inspiration and authority of the Scriptures. Rationalism and liberalism have since taken a terrible toll upon Methodism, so that most of its modern representatives bear little resemblance to their forebears.

The evangelicalism of the first half of the twentieth century also bears only shadowy comparison with the Methodists and others who figure in this book. Such evangelicals emerged somewhat flattened from their conflict with liberalism, and with little doctrinal strength. Their supposed 'Arminianism' has been more in the nature of a semi-Pelagianism, where man is required to aid God in the work of his own salvation. Modern 'Arminianism' is still of this character. In contrast, the Reformed movement of the second half of the twentieth century and the present day has doctrinal and biblical strength. But the complaint is frequently made, with some justification, that this Reformed movement is largely out of touch with the modern man and lacking in vitality. An explanation for this lies partly in the fact that the movement has been largely based on conferences rather than being rooted in local church life. There is a certain dullness about it and an intellectual exclusivity which bears little comparison with the spiritual life and vigour of New Testament Christians.

There was something about the children of the Evangelical Revival and their successors which set them head and shoulders above believers today. They knew a quality of spiritual life to which most of us are strangers. The accounts related here reflect it: a depth of spiritual experience, a joy in God, an ardent love for Christ, a thirst for holiness, a compassion for the lost and an uninhibited zeal for God. If the writing of this book gives rise to a longing for such spiritual life in those who read it, the author will feel abundantly rewarded for his labours.

In addition to owing a debt of thankfulness to many friends who have exhorted me to write this book, I am grateful to my friend Ralph Ireland for kindly reading through the manuscript to correct grammatical errors and for making helpful comments. I wish to thank other friends who have provided photographs: John Coope for the one of the ruined mill (p. 64); Marlene Stevens for those of the Redruth Wesleyan Church (p. 81) and of the Mousehole Wesleyan Church (p. 96); and the Evangelical Library for the one of Jonathan Edwards (p. 15). I owe a special debt of gratitude to Kim Cooper of the Cornish Studies Library for the provision of the photograph of Mevagissey (p. 89). My wife has been a constant encouragement and help in the work, and I owe more to her than words can tell.

Paul E. G. Cook
November 2009

See how great a flame aspires,
    kindled by a spark of grace!
Jesu's love the nations fires,
    sets the kingdoms on a blaze;
fire to bring on earth He came;
    kindled in some hearts it is:
O that all might catch the flame,
    all partake the glorious bliss!

Charles Wesley

1

REMEMBERING FORMER DAYS

The year is 1826. The location is Nottingham. The occasion, a crowded Methodist love-feast never to be forgotten by those present. Presiding was a Yorkshireman, John Smith, one of the greatest preachers ever to arise in Methodism, but whose ministry was cut short by an early death.

He led the people in earnest prayer and concluded by repeating the Lord's Prayer. The effect was extraordinary. We read that the people

> responded with peculiar fervour to each petition as it was pronounced, till he came to the doxology, at each clause of which he raised his voice and ascribed to the Almighty 'the kingdom and the power and the glory, for ever and ever' in a tone and with an unction which fell on the congregation with irresistible force.

The people were gripped with a sense of the glory of God.

> A glow of heavenly feeling pervaded the whole assembly; many
> gave vent to their emotions by bursts of tears and some with
> irrepressible shouts of praise. Others laid hold of the words,
> repeating them again and again even after he had ceased; and
> whispers of 'for ever and ever' mingled with sobs passed from
> one to another... In fact, it was some time before the regular
> business of the meeting could be resumed.[1]

We are not surprised to learn that there was an increase in the membership of the circuit that year of six hundred. God had visited his people.

Scripture encourages us to recollect such events, in order to strengthen our faith and increase our confidence in God. The Bible reminds us of the heroes of faith and urges us to keep them in mind, so that we might follow their example (Hebrews 11; 12:1). The history of God's great acts is recorded in his word, and we are exhorted to 'remember the days of old'[2] and learn from them. The Psalmists were constantly doing this to their great encouragement.[3]

Today the past is regarded as of little consequence. Modern man lives for the present and the experiences of a moment. Proven traditions and abiding principles of life are easily set aside, even in our churches, for the pleasures, fashions and sensations of the passing hour. Admittedly, to be over-absorbed with the past has its dangers, but to disregard it is folly.

Reflection upon God's actions in days gone by helps us to understand him and what he requires of us at the present time: it should encourage us to call upon him. Ignorance of former days is one of the great problems of evangelical life today. We should never forget that the Christian faith is a historic faith, anchored in the past acts of God.

The true history of the church is largely a history of revivals. As Jonathan Edwards commented:

> It may be observed that from the fall of man to our day the work of redemption in its effects has mainly been carried on by remarkable communications of the Spirit of God. Though there may be a more constant influence of God's Spirit always in some degree attending his ordinances yet the way in which the greatest things have been done towards carrying on this work always has been by the remarkable effusions at special seasons.[4]

Therefore, the most significant days in the life of the church are the days of God's power and working. The Acts of the Apostles covers one such period when the Lord Jesus Christ, though in heaven, continued his work on earth through the agency of the Holy Spirit (Acts 1:1-3). The life of the early church was marked by wave after wave of divine power, and this has been the character of the true church throughout history. Its life has been sustained by local and spontaneous spiritual awakenings resulting in its expansion and the conversion of the ungodly. It created a new social climate in the ancient world, even though the early Christians were not primarily concerned with social affairs or political considerations.

The purpose of this book is to draw attention to a series of revivals which took place in Britain during the period 1791-1840, many of which are in danger of being forgotten. But it is necessary first to consider something of the background.

Jonathan Edwards

The Evangelical Revival

The great Evangelical Revival of the eighteenth century stands out as one of the most significant epochs in the history of the church in Britain. After the long spiritual decline which followed the Restoration of the monarchy in 1660, this awakening is commonly regarded as the era when the nation was turned back to God. Larger numbers were then converted and gathered into Christ's kingdom than at any other previous time. However, this view of the Evangelical Revival is only partially correct.

The labours of those great preachers, George Whitefield, John and Charles Wesley, Howel Harris, Daniel Rowland, and men such as John Cennick, William Grimshaw, John Berridge, Martin Madan, Benjamin Ingham and others, were respons-ible under God for the conversion of thousands and for the establishment of preaching centres throughout the land. But these preachers were pioneers preparing the way for the spread of the gospel in unevangelized parts. It is not generally appre-ciated that they were relatively few in number, or that during the Evangelical Revival the testimony to the truth of the gospel was largely confined to certain parts of the country and, within these, to particular towns and villages. Daniel Rowland in Llangeitho, for example, drew his congregation from a wide area in which there was little other evangelical witness. And John Wesley's labours were mainly centred upon London, Bristol and Newcastle, with regular visits to Cornwall.

John Wesley

During the period of the Evangelical Revival, which can be dated in England from the beginning of the extraordinary ministry of George Whitefield in 1737 until the close of the era in 1791 when John Wesley died, it was not unusual for people in many towns and villages to live without the slightest awareness that any revival of true religion was in progress. The day when the generality of the nation was to be confronted with the gospel in almost every city, town and village of our land

George Whitefield

had not yet arrived. The Evangelical Revival was responsible for an extensive preaching of the gospel to ordinary working-class men and women, and resulted in large numbers being brought into the kingdom of God. The established church, however, opposed it, and the denominations of the Old Dissent — Baptists, Independents and Presbyterians — were largely unaffected by it.

The revival was one of those 'raw' periods of history, with great pioneer preachers opening up a way for the gospel and gathering together men and women who had been touched by God, forming them into little groups for spiritual fellowship and prayer. These were days when believers were frequently and brutally persecuted, and when their preachers laboured against fierce opposition, suffering much privation and hardship. The gospel was preached throughout the land, but the period of phenomenal ingathering when chapels were built and a gospel witness established in almost every town and village was still to come.

The second Evangelical Awakening: 1791-1840

The Evangelical Revival was a breaking-up of the fallow ground, but the time of intensive sowing and reaping in which the gains of the revival were consolidated came in the years 1791-1840.

Dr J. Edwin Orr's valuable book, entitled *The Second Evangelical Awakening in Britain,* first published in 1949, and dealing with the 1859-65 revival, ought to have been entitled *The Third Evangelical Awakening in Britain.* The second Evangelical Awakening in the British Isles, following the Evangelical Revival of the eighteenth century, was in the period 1791-1840. Dr Orr later revised his views and came to regard the 1859 revival as the fourth or even the fifth evangelical awakening! He had discovered the period of successive revivals from the early 1790s and extending into the 1840s, during which time spontaneous revivals were breaking out all over the British Isles in varying degrees of divine power: sometimes limited to certain towns and denominations, whilst at other times sweeping the nation.

Neglected records

Material relating to this period of early nineteenth-century revivals is largely confined to denominational histories and records. Regrettably the period was one in which denominational boundaries, drawn usually on the basis of secondary issues, were sharply defined and rarely crossed. Much information is found in the biographies of the period, but these are little known and rarely read. The records of these revivals lie buried in the literature of denominations, whose members today generally are not interested in their spiritual origins. And, in addition, denominational and theological prejudice has prevented others investigating this period. Yet this was the era when the British Isles were most effectively evangelized.

Another problem with the source material of this period is that whereas Methodism with its various strands provides considerable information through its denominational records such as *The Arminian Magazine,* started by Wesley in 1778 and later replaced by *The Methodist Magazine* in 1798, the Dissenters (Baptists and Independents), not being centrally governed, had few such records. We are left with whatever material has survived in the minute books of each church and with what is found in such sources as *The Evangelical Magazine.* This largely explains why the reader will find more reference to Methodism within these pages than to the Dissenting churches.

In this connection a further observation needs to be made. Whereas many revivals took place within Methodism, the outstanding growth of the Dissenting churches was not generally marked with spiritual movements or events of such intensity as would normally be described as 'revivals'.[5] The effects of the ministries of William Gadsby (the High Calvinist) and William Roby (the Congregationalist) in Manchester were far reaching and led to the formation of many groups and churches, but these movements, though not normally regarded as revivals, were as beneficial and long lasting in their fruits as those generally designated as such.

Decline of the Evangelical Revival and growth of rationalism

There are those who suggest that what took place in these years was a continuation of the eighteenth-century revival, as though the events of the early nineteenth century were the last movements of life as the Evangelical Revival finally expired. This interpretation in no way accords with the evidence, since the Evangelical Revival was in decline well before the death of John Wesley in 1791. Even before he died in 1770, Whitefield had complained of an absence of the old fire. The weakening of the revival influences from the 1770s onwards was accompanied in the traditional churches by an increase in Arianism and naturalistic interpretations of the Christian faith. The supernatural elements were discounted, the biblical doctrine of grace openly denied, and increasing worldliness appeared within the churches.

The established church had 'closed its doors' against the preachers of the Evangelical Revival, and the Methodist converts had suffered much persecution at the hands of the clergy. An Anglican as committed as the Countess of Huntingdon had been forced out of the church in 1782. Her Trevecca students had rarely been able to obtain ordination by the bishops. The condition of the Anglican Church at the end of the eighteenth century and into the nineteenth was dire, best summed up by the ugly word latitudinarian, with most of the clergy given over to place-seeking, worldly pleasures and pursuits, together with a general neglect of spiritual duties. The objectives of true Christianity were almost wholly absent and the abuse of privilege had become something of a normality. In his recent book *William Wilberforce: the Life of the Great Anti-Slave Campaigner*, William Hague gives a succinct summary of the conditions affecting the established church at this time.[6]

In Scotland and Ireland, scene of a powerful work of God during the Evangelical Revival, there had also been a serious spiritual decline towards the end of the eighteenth century. William Cunningham described the period as 'one of the most deplorable of the Church's history'. The ministers in Scotland were generally ignorant of biblical doctrine, negligent of their duties, and careless of men's souls. In Ireland, Arianism and other forms of infidelity prevailed, and, as one commentator expressed it, 'a dead chill rested on the Presbyterian churches of the north of Ireland, similar to that which prevailed in Scotland'. Moderatism, as it was called in Scotland, had quenched the fire of revival in both countries; and on the Continent the force of the

Great Awakening was already spent, with Socinianism reigning in the theological seminaries and poisoning the churches.

The general unhealthy condition of the churches at this time did not necessarily mean that those sections of the church which had been powerfully affected during the revival were in a similar condition. The Methodist societies in England were not tainted with the unbelief which had undermined sections of Nonconformity, such as the Presbyterian and the General Baptist churches, but towards the end of his life John Wesley was much disturbed by evidences of spiritual decline within the revival movements. The Evangelical Revival was certainly at an end by the time he died in 1791.

A new work of God

Quite apart from all this evidence, the revivals of 1791-1840 were clearly a new work of God in that many of them occurred within sections of the church which had been unaffected by the eighteenth-century revival. In Methodism they broke out following a period of spiritual stagnation, and at times, as in the case of the emergence of Primitive Methodism, the old bottles had become too brittle to contain the new wine. The early nineteenth-century awakening in Britain and on the Continent was a new spiritual movement, distinct in its origins from the Evangelical Revival which had preceded it. Yet it manifested the same glorious divine power in the arousing of sinners, in the spreading of the gospel, and in the revival of the churches.

The statistical evidence for this new work

When John Wesley died in 1791 the *Wesleyan Methodists* in Britain numbered 72,000 members with an additional half a million adherents. These mainly consisted of people who attended the services but had not openly professed conversion nor sought membership and admission to the Lord's Table. Despite divisions and secessions, the membership of the Wesleyans had increased to 245,000 by 1828, and within the next fifteen years another 100,000 were added. By 1851 there were close on 360,000 members: a fivefold increase in sixty years. The year 1851 is significant because in that year a religious census was taken throughout the UK of the numbers attending the churches.

The *Primitive Methodists* grew from a handful in 1811 to 34,000 within eighteen years. When Hugh Bourne, one of their outstanding leaders, died in 1852 their membership stood at 110,000, with an additional 230,000 adherents. These converts were not 'sheep' stolen from Wesleyan Methodism, but people mainly from the labouring classes, particularly those in the rural areas.

In the same period the *Particular* or *Calvinistic Baptists*, bypassed during the eighteenth-century revival, were delivered from the deadening influence of the High Calvinism of Joseph Hussey and John Gill, and experienced a marvellous expansion. In 1801 they had 652 places of worship, but by 1851, before the youthful Charles Spurgeon had even begun his ministry, they had increased to 2,789 chapels and 400,000 adherents. In Wales in 1790 there were forty-eight Particular Baptist chapels, most of which had been established by an unashamed process of drawing off adherents from the Calvinistic Methodist and Independent churches. A glorious converting work began, however, towards the end of eighteenth century, so that by 1851 there were 456 places of worship — a tenfold increase over sixty years.

The *Congregationalists* or *Independents*, with the notable exception of Philip Doddridge and a few others, had largely opposed the Evangelical Revival of the eighteenth century, choosing to remain detached, cool and respectable. But they were extensively revived in the early nineteenth century so that by the time of the 1851 census their estimated adherents numbered over half a million. Owen Chadwick, however, reckoned their strength as nearer three quarters of a million,[7] being especially influential in the new industrial cities and urban areas.

Social effects of the revivals

Overall, between 1791-1840, one and half million people were gathered into the Nonconformist chapels of England and Wales alone: one out of every ten of the population at that time. The explanation for this remarkable harvest is not found in a tradition of church attendance — that came later in the Victorian era — but in the extraordinary visitations of the Spirit of God which resulted in the conversion of hundreds of thousands of people of the labouring and lower-middle classes. The period was one of frequent revivals of true religion in which men and women, awakened to the realities of eternal things, sought the mercy of God freely offered in the gospel of Jesus Christ. This great work of God shaped the subsequent history of our nation, and laid the foundation for many of the reforms of the Victorian age. Referring to this era J. R. Green, in his *A Short History of the English People,* observed:

> A religious revival burst forth … which changed in a few years the whole temper of English society. The Church was restored to life and activity. Religion carried to the hearts of the people a fresh spirit of moral zeal, while it purified our literature and our manners. A new philanthropy reformed our prisons, infused clemency and wisdom into our penal laws, abolished the slave trade, and gave the first impulse to popular education.[8]

This understanding has also been reflected in the writings of other notable historians such as G. M. Young, who wrote:

The Evangelicals gave to the island a creed which was at once the basis of its morality and the justification of its wealth and power, and with the creed, the sense of being an Elect People which, set to a more blatant tune, became a principal element in Late Victorian Imperialism. By about 1830 their work was done. They had driven the grosser kinds of cruelty, extravagance, and profligacy underground. They had established a certain level of behaviour for all who wished to stand well with their fellows. In moralising society they had made social disapproval a force which the boldest sinner might fear.

By the beginning of the Victorian age the faith was already hardening into a code. Evangelicalism at war with habit and indifference, with vice and brutality, with slavery, duelling, and bull-baiting, was a very different thing from evangelicalism grown complacent, fashionable, superior.[9]

In a further comment Young touched upon an issue exercising some of our politicians today:

The Evangelical discipline, secularized as respectability, was the strongest binding force in a nation which without it might have broken up, as it had already broken loose.[10]

As we have seen, within the fifty years spanned by these virtually forgotten revivals one tenth of the population of England and Wales became associated with a Nonconformist church. The living God stretched out his arm to perform this astonishing work, a work which shaped the subsequent history of our nation for over a hundred years. It laid the foundation of all the social, educational, penal and political reforms which became so much a feature of our national life during the Victorian era. Theodore Flieder, a German pastor, who came to London in 1823 to meet Elizabeth Fry, the English prison reformer, commented:

I learned to know a whole host of institutions that minister to the bodies and souls of men. I inspected their schools and prisons. I observed their homes for the poor, and the sick and the orphaned. I studied their missionary societies and their Bible societies and their societies for the improvement of prisons, and so forth. And I particularly noted that practically all these institutions and organisations were called into being by a living faith in Jesus Christ, and that nothing but this vital faith sustains them.[11]

The revivals and the abolition of slavery

Much has been written in connection with the two hundredth anniversary of the abolition of the slave trade in 1807. Credit has rightly been given to William Wilberforce for his efforts in Parliament in support of the anti-slavery movement.

However, the traditional and popular view that Wilberforce brought about the abolition of the slave trade and was responsible for the prohibition of slavery in 1833 is hardly an accurate evaluation. Richard F. Lovelace provides a corrective in his comment that 'Although Wilberforce's inspired oratory helped reach and compel the conscience of Parliament, it is inconceivable that the work could have been accomplished without a broad base of popular sentiment supplied by the conversions and awakening throughout the English churches.'[12]

We are told that it took William Wilberforce and his friends *fifty* years to abolish slavery, from the time he first investigated the problem and then formally espoused the cause of abolition in May 1787, until the final victory in 1833. Given this long period of time, it is difficult to argue that their personal involvement was primarily responsible for the abolition. Other factors must also have been at work. The eventual end of slavery was not so much due to Wilberforce and others involved with him in the campaign, but to the humanizing influences of the evangelical gospel, which over this period had been changing the character and mood of the nation. Lord John Russell, prime minister from 1846-52 and again in 1865-66, looking back, made the following declaration: 'I know the Dissenters. They carried the Reform Bill; they carried the abolition of slavery; they carried Free Trade; and they'll carry the abolition of Church Rates.' But the real credit does not belong to Wilberforce or to the Dissenters; it belongs to the gospel and those powerful revivals of religion which created a new consensus of opinion within the country. The success of the gospel provided a sympathetic climate in which the reforms became possible.

The spiritual condition of the Anglican Church

Whereas in the Evangelical Revival of the eighteenth century the work of God took place largely within the context of the Anglican Church, in the revivals of 1791-1840 the work was almost entirely confined within the Nonconformist denominations. Most of the preachers used by God in the early days of the Evangelical Revival were ordained clergy of the Anglican Church. But in these later revivals the preachers whom God used were almost entirely Nonconformists.

One looks in vain for any great succession to men such as John Newton, Thomas Scott, Richard Cecil, Henry Venn, Isaac Milner and Charles Simeon. Much has been made of the magnificent achievements of the Clapham Sect, whose Anglican members were so influential in most of the social and political reforms achieved in the period under review. What is not so generally appreciated is that the evangelicals in the Anglican Church at this time were inclined to be diverted from their evangelistic task by over-involvement in causes espoused by the Clapham Sect, and this limited their contribution to the spread of the gospel in the early nineteenth century.

It is a strange irony that without the support of the growing number of Nonconformists who were less directly concerned with social and political issues, the Clapham Sect would have been powerless to achieve its objectives. They could have done little without the groundswell of public opinion which had been so fundamentally changed by the spread of the gospel within the dissenting denominations. Sir George Trevelyan observed: 'Without the aid of nonconformist sympathy, and money, and oratory, and organisation, their operations would have been doomed to certain failure.' [13]

The established church had become increasingly worldly towards the end of the eighteenth century, and evangelical influence within the church was in decline in the early decades of the nineteenth century. From 1833 onwards, the Oxford Movement, with its High Church emphases, was to a large extent motivated by a concern with the decline of spiritual life within the church and the growing influence of liberal theology. The launch of the Evangelical Alliance in 1846 was something of a rearguard action mainly by Anglican Evangelicals against the erosion of Protestantism within the established church. But Anglican evangelicalism was at a low ebb during this period of the revivals which brought about such an astonishing increase in the Nonconformist churches.

Wider influences

This second Evangelical Awakening assumed even greater proportions in America where the revivals of that period have not been neglected. In Europe also, Robert Haldane's Geneva lectures on Paul's Epistle to the Romans in 1816 precipitated a revival which spread from Switzerland throughout Germany, France and Holland. These movements persisted into the 1840s.

Unsubstantiated charges

Our relative ignorance of the period 1791-1840, when the greatest expansion of the church ever to take place in this country occurred, is responsible in measure for some rather misleading statements and claims often heard. It has been suggested that a full-orbed Calvinism is an obstacle to the spread of the gospel and that the belief that Christ died only for the elect is a great hindrance to evangelism. The fears for the work of God which prompt such statements are without foundation. The whole impetus of the modern missionary movement had its beginnings in the early 1790s with men who believed in a limited atonement. The Particular Baptists, as their name clearly implies, believed that Christ died only for the elect; yet they were responsible for the formation of the Baptist Missionary Society in 1792 and were later to experience an astonishing increase in their churches in the early nineteenth century.

Exactly the same was true of the Independents. They had been involved in the formation of the London Missionary Society in 1795, and were to evangelize the urban areas of England's industrial cities in the early decades of the following century. It was not the doctrine of limited atonement, a thoroughly biblical doctrine as we understand it, which had hindered the spread of the gospel. On the contrary, it was the unbiblical doctrine of eternal justification (see pp. 126-7) strongly held by many Particular Baptists and Independents which had made faith virtually superfluous and had inhibited a free offer of the gospel to sinners.

But the clearing of Calvinism from the totally unwarranted charges made against it on account of the doctrine of limited atonement ought not to allow us a spirit of complacency. From other quarters today, equally inaccurate statements are being made, such as the assertion that unless Christians embrace the Reformed doctrines there can be no hope of revival. What

God did for the Calvinistic preachers and congregations of the Baptists and Independents in 1791-1840, he also did for the Arminian believers of Wesleyan and Primitive Methodism.

However, the great revivals of 1791-1840 do contain theological lessons for us. The changes in outlook and understanding which eventually brought such blessing to the Particular Baptists and Independents illustrate how great a hindrance Hyper-Calvinism or even High Calvinism can be to the spread of the gospel. Not until the Particular Baptists came to see that the gospel was 'worthy of all acceptation' and must be freely preached to all men without inhibition, did God choose to pour out his Spirit upon them. The same was true of the Independents, who had to learn the additional lesson that human respectability and middle-class 'taste' have frequently to give way to movements of the Spirit of God.

The period also illustrates that those Arminian societies and preachers, who experienced so much of the power of God, were constantly aware that the prosperity of the gospel depends upon the sovereign visitations of God to his people, and that the salvation of the lost rests upon God proving gracious to sinners crying out for mercy. In practice, their attitudes and mentality were of such a biblical character that a more truly Calvinistic note was sounded in their spiritual life than is often heard in Reformed circles today. Despite their doctrinal inconsistencies, they believed that the spread of the gospel and the health of the church depend entirely upon the favour and power of God, and this is why they prayed so much.

This new work of God

As has been already noted, some writers regard the revivals under review as just the consolidation of the eighteenth-century Evangelical Revival. But it was clearly a *new* work. The one was essentially a pioneer movement establishing preaching centres in various parts of the country, whereas in 1791-1840 the whole nation was reached with the gospel. The evidence for this, as we have seen, is twofold.

First, the Evangelical Revival was on the wane before 1791, the year that John Wesley died. Wesley and others had complained that from the 1780s there had been a noticeable decline of spiritual zeal among the children of the revival. Secondly, the Congregationalists and Baptists were a significant force in this new revival. Their awakening did not come from contact with the Methodism of the Evangelical Revival, but from the influence of Jonathan Edwards and his writings upon their leaders.

Many church historians attribute the social reforms of the nineteenth century to the eighteenth-century revival. But the secularist effects of the French Revolution of 1789 are often overlooked, as are the strong forces of reaction it generated. Also overlooked are the rationalistic influences of the Enlightenment. The impetus of the eighteenth-century revival might well have been lost had it not been for the spiritual awakenings between 1791-1840. So we must turn to a consideration of those events which prevented this from happening.

2

THE GOD WHO HEARS PRAYER

When we investigate revivals and the great works done in the name of Christ we usually discover that behind them is found some activity of prayer. When men and women wrestle with God in prayer they are shaped by God into the sort of people he intends to use to accomplish his purposes. We can think of Martin Luther, Jonathan Edwards and Hudson Taylor and how they were fashioned by God in the secret place of personal prayer for the work they were eventually to do. William Carey was given a burden of prayer for the lost souls of India before he was aware that God intended him to be the one through whom that task would be fulfilled.

This raises the question of the purpose of prayer. It is often said that 'Prayer changes things.' But it would be more correct to say that prayer changes praying people by bringing them into line with God's purposes. And in this way prayer makes God's people fit to carry out those purposes. Prayer 'in the Spirit' (Ephesians 6:18) is the instrument through which God chooses to work to fulfil what he has planned. So it is true that there is such a thing as *prevailing* prayer: prayer that opens the door to God's power and blessings. And it is also true that if we desire to see the gospel prosper, sinners converted and the people of God caught up in a movement of the Spirit, then we must give ourselves to fervent prayer. This is how God chooses to do his work. The idea that prayer puts a sort of 'arm lock' on God to do what he never intended to do is quite wrong. Prayer does not change God, nor does it alter the purposes of God, but was greatly used by him in these revivals, as we shall see.

The Call to Prayer of 1784

Jonathan Edwards had been the primary influence behind the Scottish 'Concert of Prayer' of 1744. His *Humble Attempt to Promote Explicit Agreement ... of God's people in Extraordinary Prayer for Revival of Religion and the Advancement of Christ's Kingdom on Earth* of 1747 became the major influence behind a further such movement — the 1784 Call to Prayer.

God had used Edwards' writings to deliver the Particular Baptists from Hyper-Calvinism. John Ryland (Jr), Robert Hall (Sr), Andrew Fuller, John Sutcliffe, William Carey and others were all profoundly influenced by their reading of Edwards. In April 1784 John Erskine (1721-1803) sent Ryland a copy of Edward's *Humble Attempt.* He passed it on to John Sutcliffe of Olney who was greatly moved by it and at the June Northamptonshire Particular Baptist Association meeting in Nottingham proposed that the churches set aside the first Monday evening of each month for prayer for revival, that 'the Holy Spirit may be poured down on our ministers and churches, that sinners may be converted, the saints edified, the interests of true religion revived and the name of God glorified.'[1] The Association at that time comprised churches as far apart as Nottinghamshire and Leicestershire to the north, and Hertfordshire and Buckinghamshire in the south.

The 1784 Call to Prayer concentrated the minds of God's people upon the primary need of the churches. The Concert or Union of Prayer, as it eventually became called, was joined by the Congregationalists and by the Calvinistic and Wesleyan Methodists in Wales. As the movement gathered support, it spread to Scotland, America and Europe. All over the land a cry to God ascended to heaven for an outpouring of the Spirit upon the churches and a restoration of true religion. Carey's missionary vision arose out of the 1784 Call to Prayer; and the revivals which broke out in 1791 and continued until the 1840s all over the British Isles were surely God's answer to the fervent prayers of his people.

Bala: 1791-1794

One of the earliest answers to such intercession came in Bala, North Wales, towards the end of 1791 under Thomas Charles, minister of the Independent church in the town and later the founder of the British and Foreign Bible Society in 1804. In a letter dated 7 December 1791 he describes the scene in the town on the evening of the day the revival broke out. He tells us that 'there was nothing to be heard from one end of the town to the other, but the cries and groans of people in distress of soul.'[2] The effect of this visitation was that 'The state and welfare of the soul is become

Thomas Charles of Bala
(1755 -1814)

33

the general concern of the country. Scores of the wildest, and most inconsiderate of the people, have been awakened.'[3] He cites cases of deep conviction, so strong as nearly to drive the people mad, though on deliverance their consolation and joy were correspondingly great. In another letter written a few weeks later (26 Jan. 1792) he states that the revival in Bala was continuing,

> with great power and glory ... I can hardly believe my eyes sometimes, when I see in the chapel those, who were the most faithful servants of Satan, weeping in greatest distress, under a sense of sin and danger, and crying out for mercy.[4]

Two years later, at the beginning of 1794, in a letter written to a correspondent in Scotland, he observes that:

> In the course of the last year the almighty power of the gospel has been most gloriously manifested in different parts of our country ... Last spring there was a very great and general awakening through a very large and populous district in Caernarvonshire; in the space of three months some hundreds were brought under concern about their souls.[5]

He had earlier expressed the view

> that unless we are favoured with frequent revivals, and a strong, powerful work of the Spirit of God, we shall in great degree, degenerate, and have only a 'name to live': religion will soon lose its vigour, the ministry will hardly retain its lustre and glory; and iniquity will, of consequence, abound.[6]

In this quotation Charles gives a useful definition of revival: it is 'a strong, powerful work of the Spirit of God'. What distinguishes a revival from a more normal work of the Spirit is not the character or essence of it, but the intensity and usually the extent. The Scriptures give no support to the view that a revival is some indefinable and mystical influence. Such a notion has been responsible for a regrettable reaction in some circles to the doctrine of revival — a concept which is biblical in substance though not in name. The point Charles makes is that the life and glory of the church is dependent upon frequent quickenings of the Spirit, a view which both Scripture and history confirm.

Nottingham: 1799

The Wesleyan Methodists in England who were experiencing similar outpourings of the Spirit at that time shared this outlook. The year 1799 witnessed many revivals of religion throughout the land. A powerful work of God broke out in Nottingham under William Bramwell. A respected local preacher, Thomas Tatham, bore the following witness:

> At several of our meetings, the outpouring of the Spirit was so manifest, that a whole assembly have been wrought upon and powerfully affected at once. Such glorious displays of the Lord's omnipotent power, and of his willingness to save perishing sinners, I believe will never be forgotten by hundreds who then partook of the Divine blessing. It seemed as if the Lord was about to 'sweep the nations and shake the earth, till all proclaimed him God'.[7]

A certain John Clark of Nottingham, describing one society meeting, observed:

> Mr Bramwell engaged in prayer, when he appeared to lay such hold on the Almighty as to prevail with him for a blessing. The

glory of God descended on all the society present in such a powerful manner as I never before experienced. Many were so affected, that at the conclusion of the service, they could not come down from the gallery stairs without assistance. That was the beginning of the good days at Nottingham.[8]

During Bramwell's three years in the Nottingham circuit the societies increased by approximately 1500. William Bramwell's preaching was much used by God throughout the period 1791-1814 with revivals breaking out in a number of places where he laboured in the North of England.

Cornwall: 1799

Revivals also broke out in many parts of Cornwall in 1799. *The Arminian Magazines* for 1799 and 1800 contain some of the remarkable details. The work of God which took place throughout Methodism has generally been neglected by men of Calvinistic convictions on account of its Arminianism. But we need to remember that this spiritual movement was indeed God's work, nor should we neglect anything that is part of the activity of God. Indeed, further consideration will demonstrate that most of the theological emphases of the Methodists in this period of their history were biblical.

An anonymous writer in an article in *The Biblical Repertory and Princeton Review* of July 1861 — an impeccable Calvinistic journal — commends the Wesleyans of this period for correctly affirming:

Man's ruin by the fall; his native depravity and alienation from God; his absolute need of a Saviour, and utter inability to save himself; the necessity of regeneration by the Holy Spirit; justification, not by works, but by faith alone in the blood and righteousness of Jesus; the free offer of salvation to every human being, without money and without price; the necessity of holiness, not to merit heaven, but to become meet for it — these articles constituted the very burden of their preaching.[9]

Quickening of the Old Dissent

The Particular Baptists also experienced much spiritual quickening in the 1790s. Writing in *The Evangelical Magazine* for 1799, Samuel Pearce (1766-1799), minister of Cannon Street Baptist Church, Birmingham, commented: 'We live in a day which exhibits unequivocal tokens of revival in the Church of Jesus Christ.' The annual reports of the Baptist Associations of that period, especially in the Midlands, echo this view. Prayer meetings had multiplied and were crowded. The lost were being reached in such numbers that many meeting-houses had to be enlarged and new ones built in countless towns and villages to accommodate the people pressing into the kingdom of God. An evangelistic zeal and compassion had taken hold of Orthodox Dissent.

The Evangelical Magazine for 1806 confirms that this was also true for the Calvinistic Methodists and Congregationalists, and has frequent references to 'numerous congregations'. An illustration of this is the report that on 3 September a new chapel was opened at Wanborough in Wiltshire, drawing regular congregations of four hundred. This had come about by the open-air preaching of a Mr Mantell of Swindon during the two preceding summers.

In the 1770s and early 1780s John C. Ryland of Northampton and his son John had started services in no less than fifty Midlands villages where there had been no evangelical testimony. Similar movements began to take place in other parts of the country. The overseas vision for foreign missions was matched at home by an equal concern for the evangelization of England. In the 1790s both Baptists and Independents formed itinerant societies which sent out preachers into the towns and villages of the land where the gospel was not preached.[10] In the address given at the formation of the Baptist Itinerant Society in London in 1797, we read the following:

> In these labours let them (i.e. the preachers) keep the great object constantly in view: which is not merely to propagate a set of theological sentiments, though ever so true; much less to disseminate political opinions, or to canvass the affairs of State; but in the fear of God, with much prayer, circumspection and self-denial, to warn sinners of *the wrath to come*, to preach *the unsearchable riches of Christ* — and to render their ungodly fellow-creatures truly wise, holy and happy.

This they did to a marked degree.

Beginnings of Primitive Methodism

Similar objectives were moving Hugh Bourne and William Clowes, founders of Primitive Methodism. In *The Methodist Magazines* of 1801 onwards Hugh Bourne had read of the wonderful works of God which were taking place in America, and from these accounts he conceived the idea of holding camp meetings in England. Bourne and his friends attended the Harriseahead Chapel in Staffordshire in September 1804 where, according to Bourne, 'There

Hugh Bourne

was the greatest outpouring of the Holy Ghost I have ever known ... the greatest time of power I have ever known.'[11] It was as though Bourne and his friends had been anointed by God for a special work. From this time onwards a great revival movement began in the Potteries, leading to the first camp meeting held at Mow Cop on 31 May 1807. Wesleyan Methodism, due to growing autocratic attitudes, was unable to cope with this particular development and eventually expelled its leaders, Bourne and Clowes.

William Clowes

But God's hand was in it, and through the instrumentality of these anointed men vast numbers of working-class people were brought from darkness to light in a series of spiritual awakenings.

Cornwall: 1814-1821

Cornwall became the scene of frequent revivals of religion, particularly in the years following the Redruth awakening in 1814, described locally as 'The Great Revival' when well over twenty different towns and villages were made alive to God.[12] The year 1821 was a great year in Cornwall. We read of believers so overwhelmed with manifestations of the divine glory 'that it was some time before they had bodily strength sufficient to walk home.'[13] The revival spread rapidly in the early months of 1822; and what was then happening in Cornwall was also taking place throughout the land.

Revivals in the year 1821-22

In the 1822 Wesleyan Methodist Conference it was reported that 12,000 new members had been added to the churches. Notable outpourings of the Spirit had taken place in Durham, Sunderland, Liverpool, Leeds, Derby, Newcastle-under-Lyme, Burslem, Maidstone and Canterbury. The following record of what was taking place at Bury in Lancashire is typical:

> The Lord is reviving his work among us in this Circuit. It began among the members chiefly; and among some who had backslidden from God, and had left the Society. But it is now becoming more general; and several great sinners have been converted to God.[14]

It should be noted that this nationwide movement had been preceded by days of special humiliation and prayer within the Methodist Connexion, because they were aware that the Lord had not been with them as before. This was their consistent mentality throughout the early decades of the nineteenth century. If the work of God was languishing, then they sought by earnest prayer his sovereign intervention. They did not organize special missions, or bring in a professional evangelist, or seek the introduction of novelties. They relied on the normal regular services and life of the churches.

Revivals in Scotland

Revivals broke out in Scotland in the late 1790s under the powerful preaching of James Haldane, brother of Robert, who was involved in revival in Geneva in 1816. In 1798 and 1800 the town of Moulin had been visited by God; then the isles of Skye in 1812 and 1814, and Lewis in 1824 and 1835; but the greatest year for

Scotland was 1839, and in particular those revivals associated with the preaching of W. C. Burns at Kilsyth, Perth, Dundee and Breadalbane. They have been given considerable attention, unlike the revivals occurring at the same time in England.

Methodism: 1830-35

Revivals continued within Methodism, and were reflected in significant increases of membership between the years 1830-1835. As we have noted, though the Methodists were Arminian in theology, they had a more biblical view of how the work of God is promoted than many Reformed men have today. As soon as they sensed any decline within their churches they gave themselves to prayer as they believed that apart from divine visitations no real progress could be expected within the life of the church or prosperity for the gospel.

Revival in Stepney: 1839

The reader may have sung Andrew Reed's (1787-1862) hymn:

> Spirit Divine, attend our prayers,
> and make our hearts thy home;
> descend with all thy gracious powers,
> O come, great Spirit, come.

This hymn was first sung on Good Friday in 1829 at a gathering of Congregational ministers who had met together for prayer and intercession for revival within their churches.

Ten years later Andrew Reed experienced revival in his own church in Stepney, East London. Reed was ordained in 1811, and became the first pastor of his home church, New Road

Chapel, Stepney. This seated 800, but in the first seven years of his ministry 354 members were added to the church, and by the mid-1820s the building was unable to accommodate all the congregation. In 1828 it was proposed to build a new chapel in the Commercial Road; and this was opened as Wycliffe Chapel in 1831 with seating for 2000 — most of which was soon occupied.

The revival of 1839 really had its beginnings in the October of the previous year when Dr Reed called his nine deacons together for a time of prayer. He commented: 'We were engaged three hours, and no one felt it long. We never had a more serious meeting. To me it was a grateful omen.'[15]

New Year's Day was set aside for special humiliation and prayer. There was a quickening among the people, and after the preaching service in the evening they were reluctant to disperse, and much prayer was offered up for the unconverted. 'The prayers of the people were very tender, very earnest,' comments Reed.[16]

Wycliffe Chapel, Stepney

The spirit of prayer continued in the church. Parents gathered to pray for their children, and many of the young seriously considered their spiritual state and were brought to call upon God for mercy. In the evening service on 20 January a marked solemnity spread over all the people. 'The finger of God,' observed Reed, 'was searching the conscience; some trembled on their seat, and some bowed down their heads, overwhelmed with concern.'[17] When the hymn was given out, the spirit of concern was so great that the people were unable to sing. Andrew Reed announced that there would be a short prayer meeting for any who wished to remain. Upwards of 1000 stayed and a deep sense of awe came upon the people. Reed announced that the following evening he would be available to meet with any under spiritual concern. He was engaged from 5.00pm until 10.00pm in the evening, helped by the deacons, and even then many of those who had come could not be seen.

The work of God continued with many seeking the Lord. At the church meeting at the end of March seventy-one people were proposed for membership. Reed had seen all the candidates several times. Twenty others could have been proposed but were held back so that a true work of grace could be confirmed in their lives. The church, we read, 'was filled with silent admiration and praise.'[18]

The awakening continued throughout the summer months and until November. Andrew Reed records that since the beginning of the year 'more than three hundred persons have spontaneously seen me, separately and alone, under concern for their salvation.' And he states that, of these, over two hundred were received into membership; and that in addition he believed upwards of another one hundred had 'passed from death unto life.'[19] Most of the converts had been drawn from the immediate neighbourhood, and many had not been regular churchgoers. None had come from other churches.

The converts were of all ages: from children under twelve to people as old as seventy. Regular churchgoers had been converted and backsliders had been restored. The whole work was marked by a deep sense of sin and great seriousness towards God.[20]

There are some important lessons to be learnt from this period of revivals.

1. Reformed doctrine without reformed life and conviction is powerless.

Reformed doctrine does not guarantee 'complete dependence upon God' — but such is the essence of the Reformed faith; and unless we act upon the principle and live by it then we are a contradiction of our own doctrine. The Wesleyan Methodists in the period 1791-1840 expressed that complete dependence upon God — that is why they prayed so much, and why they resorted to God whenever they sensed a decline in their churches. They believed that without God nothing is possible. The phrase 'our outreach', used so often in our churches today, would have disturbed them. They looked for *God's* outreach! They sought to work where God was working.

Surprisingly, practical Arminianism first began to express itself within the Reformed denominations such as the Particular Baptists and Independents. In the late 1830s the churches, though still retaining their Calvinistic doctrine, began to look much more to men and means than to God. The *Northern Baptist* magazine for 1839 makes frequent reference to 'revival meetings' being held in such locations as Surrey Chapel, London, scene of the outstanding ministry of Rowland Hill until 1833; and in Tottenham, Hull, Bridlington, Shrewsbury, Derby and other towns and villages. The following entry is fairly representative:

Revival Meetings. A series of meetings have been held in the village of Foston, near Gosport, for the promotion of a religious revival.[21]

The influence of the thinking and lectures of Charles Finney in *Revivals of Religion* (1835) was evidently being felt. Whereas the Methodists retained the conviction that only God could save sinners and revive churches, the Calvinists were beginning to entertain the notion that God could not be expected to do it without the employment of special means. These reports make it clear that they were also beginning to think that churches can experience a revival whenever they want it by fulfilling certain conditions. This was Finney's teaching. The irony is that it began to be entertained by Calvinistic churches well before those of Arminian persuasion. Whilst the Methodists were still seeking to 'pray down' revival in the tradition of Jonathan Edwards and according to Scripture, the Calvinists were resorting to 'special means' to work up revivals. The loss of spirituality tends to turn us all into natural Pelagians. We shall have cause to refer to this development again.[22]

2. *The work of God can only be carried on by outpourings of the Spirit*

Reaction against the Charismatic Movement has caused many to lose sight of this important principle. Jesus received the Spirit 'without measure' (John 3:34). But the church has not received the Spirit 'without measure'. Not even at Pentecost was the Spirit given in this way. The early Christians had to pray for fresh supplies of the Spirit; an example of this is recorded in Acts 4. But each new effusion had Pentecostal characteristics. The Spirit is given to the church by measure because we cannot be trusted with the power without measure. We are kept, therefore, in a position of entire dependence upon God. So we have to keep coming and calling upon God for fresh effusions of the Spirit. The preacher has to do it every time he preaches. Paul describes it as 'the supply of the Spirit of Jesus Christ' (Philippians 1:19) and such is characteristic of every work of God, whether or not we call it 'revival'.

Believers in the period 1790s-1840s understood this. The Baptists and Congregationalists had been taught by Jonathan Edwards. The Methodists, too, understood it, and the Wesleys had learnt it from Edwards — who of course learned it from the Scriptures. So they kept humbling themselves; kept calling upon God; kept coming to God like little children, 'asking, seeking, knocking' (Luke 11:9-13). God's power and blessing is not secured merely by a reformation of the church, nor just by sound doctrine. A reformed church and a reformed Christian can be most unattractive unless the dew of the Spirit is resting upon them. We must seek this heavenly dew and these divine influences in every part of our church life and in all our spiritual activities. When God hears our prayers and we receive a quickening of the Spirit, it may not occur to us that it is of the same essence as what is called 'revival'. The fact that it is limited to one place or occasion will prevent us from doing so; nevertheless it will have the same characteristics: an awareness of God's presence, deep conviction of sin and true repentance, an awe of God and holy joy and gladness in his presence. This is what marked the period 1791-1840.

3. *The beneficial social impact of the church is a consequence of the preaching of the evangelical gospel and the outpourings of the Spirit.*

It was so in the early church (cp. Acts 2:41-47). Concern for the poor and needy in the church was an effect of the gospel and of changed lives. The task of the church is not political or social, but spiritual. Real social change can only be effected as the result of spiritual change. The modern slogan 'Make poverty history', popularized by the media and some pop stars, is an impossible aspiration which has no more prospect of being realized than an expectation that selfishness, greed and avarice can be eliminated from life. Jesus said, 'The poor you have with you always' (John 12:8), because that is one of the inevitable consequences of sin. This does not mean that Christians should be indifferent to social needs; but it does underline the primary function of the church: the declaration of the Word of God.

It was the revivals of the first half of the nineteenth century which led to the social changes of the latter half. Let us not lose sight of our priorities therefore; and let us not be intimidated by liberal theology, nor by those evangelicals who have recently become 'burdened' by a social conscience, so being diverted from our real task: the preaching of the gospel. But let us call upon God for divine outpourings and supplies of the Spirit without which our preaching or any of our labours in the name of Christ will accomplish very little.

3

EARLY REVIVALS IN THE MIDLANDS AND THE NORTH OF ENGLAND

Until more recently one could not travel through the North of England without being impressed by the tremendous impact of Nonconformity upon the area. The real explanation of the great influence of 'chapel' upon the people is found in the revivals of religion which broke out in countless towns and villages in past days.

Little is known about them today, but the explanation of the numerous and frequently large chapel buildings — many of which are now derelict or have been demolished — lies in the wonderful works of God which brought most of them into being. The main lesson to be learnt from such evidences is found in Zechariah 4:6: '"Not by might nor by power, but by My Spirit," says the LORD of hosts.'

Unfortunately the Nonconformists forgot the lessons of their origins and towards the end of the nineteenth century complimented themselves for the far-reaching effects of the Christian faith upon the lives of the people. They also became proud of their political clout and of the influence of the Nonconformist

vote. Some elaborate chapel buildings erected in the period 1870-1910
appear to be monuments to human
pride rather than humble acknowl-
edgements of the grace and power of
God, unlike the earlier and much sim-
pler Nonconformist chapels.

We must consider some of the
revivals which gave rise to the amazing
increase in the number of believers
in the period 1791-1840. As we have
seen, it was a period of revivals in the
nation as a whole.

Writing of Methodism in 1790-1850
in his *History of English Nonconformity,*
Henry W. Clark comments:

Methodist church
erected in 1905

> Wesley's successors were essentially Wesley's own men, and
> conjure up the vision of Methodism wielding the old weapons
> and finding that their edge was still unblunted ... believing in
> the old spiritual powers and finding that they did not put those
> that trusted in them to any shame. Indeed, direct testimony is
> available as to how in respect of religious fruitfulness Yorkshire
> was found to be 'a land of Goshen', and as to how from that
> northern county down to Cornwall in the south the old fires
> kindled still when the old torches were applied.[1]

He is referring, of course, to the tried and proven means of
believing prayer and the preaching of the evangelical message.
Other writers observed:

> Neither preachers nor people were content with steady, slow
> progress. They were grateful for this, but they looked for, and
> obtained, times of refreshing from the presence of the Lord.[2]

As we have already noted, this period of revivals was distinct from the Evangelical Revival of the eighteenth century — though built upon it. The Dissenters (i.e., the Baptists and the Congregationalists), for example, were little affected by the Evangelical Revival, yet in the period 1791-1840 they were wonderfully revived and experienced amazing growth — the Congregationalists mainly in the new urban areas, whilst the Baptists also had great influence in the rural areas.

In 1798 Samuel Pearce of Cannon Street Baptist Church, Birmingham, sensed approaching revival in the Baptist churches and wrote:

> Prayer meetings in numerous places are well-attended; yea, better than ever. A few societies, and but a few, have their membership lessened. Some have great reason to mourn, whether they do or not, their lukewarmness and barrenness. But revivals have been enjoyed elsewhere, and the members in several churches have been more than trebled within five years, in one church a hundred were added in two years. All five churches in our little Country Association have been under the necessity of enlarging their places of worship. More of our Meeting Houses have been enlarged within the last five years, and more built within the last fifteen, than have been built or enlarged for thirty years before. Within a small time about a hundred persons have been sent into the regular work of the Ministry, and one of our churches has had the joy of introducing four the same day into the sacred service [almost certainly his own]. Multitudes of other brethren are employed according to their abilities in village services...[3]

What caused this remarkable growth amongst the Congregationalists and the Baptists? They had awoken from the deadening influence of Hyper-Calvinism, largely due to the liberating effect of the writings of Jonathan Edwards, and had caught a vision of what God intended for the gospel.[4]

We have already referred to the 1784 Call to Prayer issued by the Northamptonshire Particular Baptist Association to which there had been a significant response. God was answering the cry of his people and the resulting series of revivals, breaking out in different parts of the country throughout the period 1791-1840, did more to evangelize this land than had been achieved during the Evangelical Revival of the eighteenth century.

Before the Evangelical Revival there were only twenty-eight Congregational churches in Yorkshire. Between 1760 and 1800 some thirty-three new causes were founded. But between 1800 and 1830 sixty-six new chapels were built doubling the number of congregations in that county.[5]

When we dig back into history we discover some 'stones', and if we ask our fathers, 'What are these stones?' (Joshua 4:21), then we shall learn, like the children of Israel of old, that God had mightily visited his people. And when we discover that the very streets of the towns and cities that we now tread once rang with praises to God, we should be encouraged to call on God again to revive his work. This writer will never forget the day when he first read that in 1858 the people of Hull used to run to their places of worship — many of which seated over 1000 — in order to secure a seat for the mid-week preaching meeting. This seems inconceivable today; but it did happen, and by the grace of God we trust it will happen again. Once more we learn that it is '"Not by might nor by power, but by My Spirit," says the LORD of hosts.'

The work of Oliver Heywood, William Mitchel and David Crosley

Subsequent to the Great Ejection of 1662 a number of congregations of Presbyterian character were brought into being in Lancashire and Yorkshire through the itinerant labours of the godly Oliver Heywood. Also in this same period Baptist churches were established in those same counties through the preaching of William Mitchel and David Crosley. However, it seems that by the 1730s these churches had lost much of their spiritual vitality. Their quickening was to come in the 1790s onwards.

The awakenings under Benjamin Ingham and William Grimshaw

Turning to the influence of Methodism, we discover that Yorkshire was greatly affected during the Evangelical Revival. Benjamin Ingham, a former member of a group of Oxford students known as the 'Holy Club', established some fifty to eighty preaching centres in the West Riding. And the herculean labours of William Grimshaw of Haworth in the period 1742-63

Haworth church in Grimshaw's time

were mightily used by God for the spread of the gospel in the North of England. Before the work of Grimshaw and Ingham, the North of England had been among the most benighted areas of our land. These men were pioneers and upon the foundation of their labours the kingdom of God was established.

The beginnings of a new work of God

The Call to Prayer of 1784 had led to a considerable increase of spiritual life within the churches. Prayer meetings in the Baptist and Congregational chapels were thronged, as the quotation from Samuel Pearce confirms,[6] and earnest prayer, coupled with a new evangelistic zeal, led to the formation of many new congregations. Before the end of the eighteenth century these Dissenting chapels were crowded, and within the next twenty years the number of their places of worship doubled. They had learnt from Jonathan Edwards that revivals are called down from heaven by importunate prayer, and not worked up by men. So they called upon God in their great need, and God heard their cry.

Dewsbury: 1792

The outlook of the Wesleyan Methodists was the same; they too were experiencing revivals of religion at that time. William Bramwell was one of the most powerful of their preachers during the 1790s and the first two decades of the nineteenth century. A man of ardent prayer, his life and ministry is a challenge to any minister of the gospel. This man became God's instrument in a great revival which broke out in Dewsbury in 1792. He had been fervently praying for revival when a remarkable assurance was given him, which he recorded in his journal.

As I was praying in my room, I received an answer from God in a particular way, and had the revival discovered to me in its manner and effects. I had no more doubt. All my grief was gone; I could say, 'The Lord will come; I know he will come, and that suddenly.'[7]

Soon afterwards he describes how a remarkable spirit of prayer was given to the people. Then God came, indeed! His records describe what happened.

Several who were the most prejudiced were suddenly struck, and in agonies groaned for deliverance ... The work continued in almost every meeting... Our love-feasts began to be crowded, and people from every neighbouring circuit visited us. Great numbers found pardon, and some perfect love. They went home and declared what God had done for them.[8]

In one period of twelve weeks almost a hundred new members were added to the society, and the effect of this work of God spread throughout the area. 'Many believers were quickened, and excited to greater diligence and activity in the work of the Lord.'[9]

Birstall: 1792-94

In 1793 Bramwell was appointed to labour in the Birstall circuit, near Dewsbury, where a revival had begun during the previous year. At the Christmas love-feast the Spirit was poured out in an unusual manner. Many were awakened and not less than fifty 'obtained redemption through the blood of Jesus Christ'.[10] Their subsequent godly living confirmed the genuineness of this saving work. In the Easter of 1794 another fifty or so were converted. All the chapels in the circuit and the private houses of believers were crowded with people of all social classes as they sought the mercy of God. Within the two years that Bramwell was in the Birstall area the society membership doubled, and many others were brought under deep conviction of sin. Thomas Pearson of Gomersal provided details of this work of God as it affected his own village.

William Bramwell

> Mr Bramwell came to us full of faith and of the Holy Spirit. His powerful preaching and fervent prayers were so mighty through faith that the stoutest-hearted sinners trembled under him. Before that time we had a partial outpouring; but a mighty shower then descended, and the truth and power of God wonderfully prevailed. My class soon increased to sixty members; and all ranks and degrees of men began to attend the preaching. Every place of worship in the neighbourhood was crowded. Young persons of only ten years of age were clearly awakened and savingly converted.[11]

Revival broke out again in this area in 1812.

Revival in Hull and district: 1793

Alexander Mather gives an account of a revival in Hull in 1793.[12] God had blessed the Methodist society in Hull, he tells us, 'with much peace and unity' and growth in spiritual life. Under his preaching some had been aroused from their spiritual slumbers; but when they heard of what God was doing in the West Riding, where hundreds and even thousands have lately been awakened and converted; a very earnest desire was kindled in the hearts of the people, especially among the leaders for a revival in our society, and which impelled us to address the Throne of Grace, both in public and private, with ardent importunity.

This quickening in prayer was such that some who had never prayed in public before began to take part. 'It was very evident the Lord was carrying on a great work among the people in general, as well as in the members of the society.' He continues:

On Sunday the 9th of March, after Mr Brown had done preaching, the prayer meeting began, and concluded at the usual time. But some who were in great distress would not depart from the place; they were therefore convened in the vestry, and several of our brethren assisted them by their supplications to the Fountain of Mercy till four or five persons obtained divine peace and consolation. This being noised abroad, excited great expectations in the minds of many who felt the burden of their sins, and they came to the chapel on Monday evening... There were many, in great anguish of mind, in different parts of the chapel, and these required help as well as others; which obliged the brethren to pray with them, and encourage them to look unto the Lord for his promised salvation. In a short time, several who had been in great agony, found the blessing of forgiving mercy, and instantly rising up, declared what the Lord had done for their souls; and their friends who were around them, united together in praising the Lord in their behalf; while others, in different parts of the chapel still remained in distress. In this manner they continued till about ten persons found the Lord...

Next evening, after the public prayer meeting, many who were groaning for redemption, retired into the vestry, and continued several hours in fervent supplication; about twelve persons found peace before they departed. In this manner the work went on during the first fortnight; at every prayer meeting ten or twelve persons, and sometimes more, being brought out of darkness into the light of God's reconciled countenance, and some were likewise awakened at the same time...[13]

The account describes how the revival spread to Beverley, the capital town of the East Riding of Yorkshire, eight miles from Hull:

On the 23 of March, Mr Grant kept a love-feast at Beverley; many of our friends from Hull were present, and spoke freely of the great things which the Lord had done for their souls; the brethren at Beverley were much revived and two or three were brought into liberty. The same evening, our meeting at Hull was accompanied with much of the divine presence, and a greater number found peace than on any former occasion.[14]

The spiritual quickening increased with as many as twenty to thirty finding peace with God at every prayer meeting. In the second week of April upwards of one hundred and fifty were added to the society, having been awakened and converted. One prayer meeting continued all night, not by design, but on account of the power of God. We read:

April: 13, we had our Love-feast: Many of the new converts, stood up before the congregation, and gave a clear and satisfactory account of the work of God upon their hearts. The meeting continued till five o'clock, and it was then with reluctance that they departed. The chapel was crowded with deeply serious hearers at six o'clock, and the prayer meeting began as soon as the preaching concluded, and continued till ten, when the congregation was dismissed a second time, and they were entreated to return home, especially all whose family affairs required their attendance. But this requisition had very little effect, for the greater part continued in prayer till one or two o'clock; and even some remained till the morning preaching. About twenty found peace. At this meeting were present many of our friends from the country societies, whose souls the Lord abundantly blessed; they returned home greatly rejoicing and praising God for the things they had heard and seen.[15]

And so the revival spread to the surrounding area and 'in a few weeks some hundreds were convicted and converted'. Mather mentions Beverley 'where there had been great deadness for a long season', but where 'twenty persons have lately found peace with God. Some of them were not only strangers, but enemies to godliness.'[16]

On Good Friday, 18 April, there was prayer and preaching in the morning and preaching again at 6.00pm followed by a prayer meeting.

The prayer meeting continued till ten o'clock, which was indeed solemn and lively, and several were delivered from the burden of sin. The congregation was then dismissed, but a large number remained in every part of the chapel, as well as in the vestry, in great distress. When these were released from their troubles, more and more fell under conviction, which unavoidably lengthened the meeting to a very late hour… And many who had been delivered but a few days, or perhaps a few hours, now became earnest and prevailing intercessors for others. Even some who had ignorantly inveighed against this extraordinary work, and represented it as a scene of confusion and disorder, were constrained themselves, by the mighty power of God, to cry out for mercy as well as others.[17]

Alexander Mather informs us that 'the work continued to prosper in this remarkable manner till 12 May, considerable numbers being deeply wounded and graciously healed'.

Again, in Hull in 1794, a deep sense of sin and an awe of God came upon the people. Seventy were added to the Wesleyan society in three days under a spontaneous work of the Spirit, and in the following week upwards of another one hundred and fifty. The population at that time was little more than 15,000, and yet within the space of a few weeks hundreds were convicted and converted in Hull and the surrounding district. Eventually the work of God in Hull was so extensive that Rowland Hill was to describe the city as 'the garden of the Lord.'

4

DAYS OF THE SON OF MAN IN YORKSHIRE

The years 1792-1795 were 'days of the Son of Man' in Yorkshire generally. Many believers in the Leeds, Halifax, Bradford and Huddersfield circuits looked back to that era as the time of their union with Christ.

Sheffield: 1793-97

Under the preaching of John Moon and Alexander Mather in Sheffield, 'the presence and power of God was unusually felt, and there was a cry among the people'. Prayer meetings multiplied and people were regularly converted in them. John Moon describes a meeting held in the chapel when a woman was brought under such distress of soul that she began to cry aloud for mercy. The Methodists in Sheffield at that time were not used to this sort of thing. Moon himself was unwilling to entertain anything which interrupted the normal order. Reluctantly he handed over the conduct of the meeting to the local preachers and made his way to the gallery to deal with the distressed soul. He recounts that after a hymn one of the local preachers engaged in prayer, at which instant, 'the power of God in a wonderful manner filled the place. The cries of the distressed instantly broke out like a clap of thunder from every part of the chapel'[1] drowning the voice of the man who prayed. All over the chapel, sinners were crying out for mercy and finding the salvation of God, so that 'cries for mercy and thanks for pardoning love, ascended in a wonderfully mixed, but grateful incense, before the heavenly throne'.[2] All normal procedures had to be set aside as the curious made their way to the chapel to witness this astonishing work of God, many of whom were themselves seized with conviction as soon as they entered. The meeting continued until two in the morning; and John Moon estimated that as many as seventy found peace with God. The work continued with very great power for three days during which

…one hundred persons or upwards, struggled into the gracious kingdom of our God and Saviour; besides a number that were now alarmed with a sense of their danger; husbands and wives, parents and children, masters and servants, not knowing the change that had taken place in each other; during these opportunities, we exulted together in the love of God, and admired the power of changing grace.[3]

William Bramwell was appointed by the July 1794 Conference to the Sheffield circuit. Under his ministry the revival continued and increased in power. James Sigston, his biographer, describes the effect of his labours:

The embers of love were kindled all around: when he visited the societies, he found them 'striving together for the furtherance of the Gospel'. Opposition was broken down, lukewarmness was destroyed, and a holy vision was maintained, and the work of God in the town and country broke out in a flame of life, and power, and zeal ... wherever he went, visible signs and wonders were wrought in the name of Christ: and in the course of the first year, twelve hundred and fifty members were added to the society![4]

In the following two years 1795-1797, as many as seventeen to eighteen hundred were added to the society. It has to be remembered that the population of Sheffield at that time would have been barely 30,000. So amazing was this work of God that people came from many different parts of England to witness it.

In 1794 thousands were awakened and converted in the West Riding of Yorkshire. Revivals broke out in almost every society in the Leeds circuit, where two thousand new members were added in that one year alone. In Halifax seven hundred professed conversion and were able to give clear and distinct accounts of the work of God upon their souls.

William Bramwell, who had been greatly used by God in the Nottingham revival of 1798-1801, was appointed to the Leeds circuit in 1801. Revival broke out again under his preaching. Within the first year the membership of the society increased by 371 members. The surrounding area was even more powerfully awakened than Leeds itself. Bramwell, writing from Leeds to a friend, Rev. Zechariah Taft, on 30 November 1802, was able to comment:

We had such a work in one street as I have seldom seen; many amongst those who were the worst are now become the best.[5]

No doubt the reader can think of notorious streets and estates in his own area over which he would rejoice to report a similar happening. Humanly speaking, it is inconceivable, but let us not forget how God works. Again, it is '"Not by might nor by power, but by My Spirit," says the LORD of hosts.'

Revivals in Bradford, Keighley and Yeadon

In the autumn of 1805 an outpouring of the Spirit took place among the Methodists in Bradford. We are told 'the doors of the octagon chapel were scarcely ever closed for more than ten weeks by day or night, often a full congregation retiring to find an equally large company awaiting entrance.'[6] Nine hundred new members were received into fellowship before the year's end. Early in the following year, 1806, revival broke out in the Keighley district of Yorkshire. And at Yeadon, near to where the Leeds and Bradford airport is now situated, the local chapel was soon filled with three or four hundred people calling upon God in prayer. Five hundred were added to the society at Yeadon alone in that one year. Wonderful are the works of God!

The early days of Primitive Methodism

In 1807 the early beginnings of Primitive Methodism had taken place at Mow Cop in Staffordshire where their first camp meeting was held. There were some mighty men of prayer amongst them. One of these was a quaint character from the East Riding of Yorkshire by the name of John Oxtoby. Born in 1767 near Pocklington, he had lived for thirty-seven years hating religion and indulging himself in every form of wickedness. But in 1804 he was awakened and came under a terrible conviction of sin. After suffering great agonies of soul he was wonderfully converted. In 1824 he entered the work of God full time, and we are told he did so 'like a boxer wanting to give a knock-out blow to Satan.' Much could be written about this remarkable man who became known as 'Praying Johnny'[7] because, as Joseph Ritson expressed it, 'His power lay in the spiritual realm and there he was indeed a prince of God. Six hours each day he usually spent on his knees and in this way he girded himself for his amazing conquests.'[8]

One of the most memorable of these was the manner in which he 'took' Filey for the Lord by prayer in 1823. Filey, a fishing village in the East Riding, was noted for its wickedness and pagan practices. Attempts had been made to establish a work there by the Primitive Methodists in Bridlington, but the work had proved fruitless and a proposal was made to abandon it. John Oxtoby objected. 'What will the people say about praying and believing?' he interjected. 'Let me go.' When he reached Muston Hill and viewed Filey in the distance, he fell upon his knees in a dry ditch and began to agonize with God. A miller passing that way thought he heard two men arguing. But it was only one man praying. He was engaging in 'the argument of faith' with his God. Eventually God gave Oxtoby the assurance that his prayers were answered. He 'rose in faith' and exclaimed, 'It is done, Lord! It is done! Filey is taken! Filey is taken!' So he descended into the town: and it was taken!

Ruined mill off Muston/Filey road
near the place where Oxtoby prayed for Filey

Oxtoby believed that 'the Lord gave me eighty souls while I was praying in the ditch this morning.' He preached through the village and in the house of a Mrs Gordon, the wife of a coastguard officer and 'one of the most remarkable and useful women Primitive Methodism produced.'[9]

John Oxtoby's grave

Fifty of the eighty were saved. A great revival swept the town which completely transformed its moral and spiritual tone and laid the foundations of a powerful church which continued in strength into the twentieth century.[10] Many of the fisher folk became shining examples of virtue in contrast to the slaves of vice which once they had been.

The statistics of the forty societies of Primitive Methodism in the Yorkshire Wolds, published fifty years later, gives the membership of the Filey society as 269, with a regular congregation of 600 — as large as the Beverley congregation. Such is the power of true revival.

The widespread revivals of 1821

As we have observed, the general outlook of the Wesleyan Methodists in the early decades of the nineteenth century, before Charles Finney's ideas began to influence evangelical life in this country, was that when the work of God languished they needed to seek by earnest prayer a sovereign intervention of God.

In the period 1816-1820 the Wesleyan Methodists saw an increase in membership of only one per cent each year, far less than the population growth. They knew something was wrong — the blessing and manifest presence of God had departed from them. They called a fast day for special humiliation and prayer for the revival of the work of God.[11] This was followed in 1821 by a widespread revival which added 9,000 members to their churches. *The Methodist Magazine* of 1821 reported extensive revivals throughout the country. In Liverpool thirty to fifty conversions were taking place weekly; and in Sunderland a great reviving had added many to the societies — one chapel alone received one hundred new members. In the following year, 1822, at the Methodist Conference it was reported that 12,000 new members had been added to the churches.

In the early 1820s local spontaneous revivals in Baptist, Congregational and Methodist churches were so numerous that they ceased to be reported as unusual events. God had come to his people in answer to their prayers.

The Yeadon revival: 1834

The Methodist Magazine of 1834 contains a report of another extraordinary revival which began in Yeadon, near Leeds, a town that had known revival twenty-eight years earlier in 1806.[12] By the end of January 1834, the whole community had come under a wonderful sense of the presence of God. Conviction of sin was so widespread that business was suspended for several days in some of the workplaces. People were weeping in the streets over their sins. So great was the number of penitent souls that prayer meetings were held from morning to night in the chapel. The movement spread to Guiseley and Rawden. Six hundred were converted in Yeadon; two hundred and fifty in Guiseley; and one hundred in Rawden. The population of these places at the time totalled 5,600 of whom over 900 were converted in this revival, and added to the churches.[13]

Samuel Wilde, superintendent minister of the Yeadon circuit at this time, wrote on 20 September 1834 to Jabez Bunting, the outstanding Methodist leader of that period:

> You have heard no doubt of the great revival of the work of God in this town and circuit for which I hope we shall never cease to be thankful to God. Such has been the addition to our numbers that our old Chapel will not hold the whole of the members of our Society by some hundreds so that we have been obliged to build a new Chapel...
>
> Our Trustees have unanimously desired me to give you a pressing invitation to open our chapel... Do come and see 'the Grace of God' and I am sure you will be glad. I am happy to say that the great majority of our new converts stand fast and we are expecting to have the whole town converted when we get our new chapel opened. As our people are nearly all poor our strength is in our numbers, but, as trade has been very bad in this neighbourhood since we began the erection of our chapel until very lately, many small subscriptions which were then promised will not be obtained for some time to come, so that it is the more necessary that we should have a good opening. Everything considered our people have done wonders so that we hope to have our chapel placed in good circumstances...
>
> It is a pleasing fact that our revival has led already to the erection of four new chapels and the enlargement of several more.[14]

He seems not to have been successful in securing the services of Jabez Bunting, because eighteen months later another letter was sent to Dr Bunting from the new superintendent minister, Samuel Robinson, headed 'Yeadon, near Leeds, 16 April 1836', in which he states:

...We have six hundred members in this village; not the like, perhaps, to be found in the whole connexion of the same amount of population; and our congregations command, with very few exceptions, the whole adult inhabitants. They are an excellent people...[15]

What we cannot achieve in a lifetime, despite all our efforts and labours, God can do in a few days when he chooses to come amongst us with great power.

Northern Baptists and the Finney effect

Christians in the early decades of the nineteenth century believed in the necessity of revivals. *The Northern Baptists* — a magazine issued by the Particular Baptists and to which we have already made reference — makes interesting reading for the year 1839. Quotations from a book on *The Necessity of Revivals* by J. Douglas are printed,[16] of which the following are significant:

With regard to vital and inward religion, we may lay it down as a maxim which cannot deceive us, that where there is no revival, there must be decay.

A religion that rests upon form and custom can have no permanence.

The magazine carries a number of excellent articles by the Rev. B. Evans of Ebenezer Baptist Church, Scarborough, a minister of some considerable influence, written in the form of letters to the editor, the Rev. R. Harness of Bridlington, in which he deals with 'The State of the Denomination'. He examines the condition of the Baptist churches in the East and North Ridings of Yorkshire and complains that they are not as prosperous and converts not as numerous as formerly. He quotes Andrew Fuller to the effect that 'Our want of usefulness is often to be ascribed to our want of spirituality, much oftener than to our want of natural ability.'

But the magazine presents a strange shift of emphasis from God to man. It reports what it calls 'Revival Meetings' being held in different parts of the country in Congregational and Particular Baptist churches for 'the promotion of a religious revival'. As we have already noted, one senses the influence of Charles G. Finney in these developments, with the belief that revivals can be 'worked up' by man.[17] Finney's *Lectures on Revivals of Religion* (1835) is quoted with approval.[18] Commendatory remarks are made on his sermons under *Notice of Books*, though some 'defects' are admitted.[19] All this indicates that Finney's influence was having a marked effect on English Calvinists even at this early stage. Yet despite the fact that these Particular Baptists had clearly been affected by his teaching, at least it can be said of them that they still believed that the work of God can only be effectively advanced by revivals of religion.

We must learn afresh, however, that 'though we walk in the flesh' we cannot war after the flesh. 'For the weapons of our warfare are not carnal but mighty in God for pulling down strongholds' (2 Corinthians 10:4). So let us again resort to our spiritual weapons: faith, prayer, preaching and letting loose among men of God's almighty gospel. What we must learn from all these revivals is the principle we referred to at the beginning, that of Zechariah 4:6 — the work of God can only be carried on by the power of the Spirit.

Isaac Marsden (1807-1882) from Skelmanthorpe, much used by God in revivals at Market Rasen during 1837 and Wigan in 1846, writing in 1878 on the need of the power of the Spirit within Methodism, commented:

I say, my brother, it won't do to be content with giving first-rate sermons without being endowed with power from on high. The world will give its applause and hurrahs, and foolish preachers may be pleased with the honour; but it will go out like a falling star.[20]

And in a letter written in 1880 he observed:

There is a great deal of talk about, 'What is to be done to raise Methodism?' My answer is: Only *one thing* for the pulpit and the pew. Not a splendid ritual, nor splendid chapels, nor splendid sermons, nor splendid concerts, nor splendid lectures nor bazaars. *The Pentecost is that one thing* for the pulpit and the pew. All other things *without this* are splendid sins, and splendid professions, and splendid shams.[21]

In our desperate situation today we need to cast ourselves upon God. We are not as *desperate* as we ought to be. Depressed, perhaps; but that is because we have been too self-assured, overconfident in ourselves and our schemes. We do not cast ourselves upon God like our forefathers. Despite our professions, our Reformed theology is too much in our heads and too little in our hearts. The truth of the matter is that we are not Reformed enough. Despite their doctrine, the mentality of the old Methodists was much more Reformed than ours. They depended upon God more than we do, they looked to him more often, they prayed more diligently. In the sort of situation that faces us today, they had but one answer: call upon God. And this they did again and again.

5

CORNWALL AND THE GREAT REVIVAL OF 1814

In times of spiritual decline Christians should not fail to do two things. The first is to humble ourselves before God. This is what Isaiah (Isaiah 6), Ezra (Ezra 9), Nehemiah (Nehemiah 1) and the children of Israel (Nehemiah 9) all did. Then secondly, we should remember the former days when God has visited his people. This is what the Psalmists did. In Psalm 44:1-3 the Psalmist looks back to days when God came to the rescue of his people and acted on their behalf. We find this again in Psalm 77:5-6,10-15 where the Psalmist reflects upon past days and is encouraged to call upon God for divine interventions.

We learn that it was the practice for one generation to speak to another of the former mighty acts of God; and this recital became the occasion of renewed faith and prayer for spiritual restoration. The knowledge of what God has done in previous days ought to be sufficient to save us from despair and renew our hope in God. We should be interested therefore in these glorious revivals of the past. We must be careful, however, not to adopt an attitude of passivity as though there were nothing we can do to promote the conditions which favour revival, conditions such as repentance and a thirsting after God.

Billy Bray and William Haslam

General awareness about revivals in Cornwall appears to be confined mainly to those revivals in which Billy Bray was involved in 1848-51 and 1851-54. *The King's Son, A Memoir of Billy Bray* by F. W. Bourne has been the main source of popular knowledge about Billy Bray. But a much more significant book, giving a detailed account of the revival at Baldhu in 1851-54, is entitled *From Death into Life* by William Haslam, a man converted under his own preaching, and greatly used by God as the main instrument in that awakening. The book has been republished in recent days. William Haslam had been caught up in the High Church Oxford Movement whilst he was an undergraduate at the university, and with great religious zeal went to Cornwall in 1842 to 'convert' the Cornishmen. He discovered that their souls needed far more than the elevating influence of religious art and the beauty of religious buildings and elaborate ritual. To the ordinary Cornishman the 'holiness of beauty' — so much an emphasis of the Tractarian Movement — seemed to have little appeal. Haslam discovered that there could be no substitute for the power of the new birth, which he himself experienced in 1851, or for the message of justification by faith which he preached thereafter.

Up until the 1960s the Cornish people were inclined to regard themselves as quite distinct from the generality of English people. Their temperament, history and culture set them apart from the rest of the country. Their Celtic origin and geography isolated them within the nation from the social and political influences which prevailed elsewhere.[1] And to some extent the revivals of religion gave rise to spiritual expressions of religious life with a character all of its own. This becomes evident in the accounts which follow.

Early days and the preaching of the Wesleys

The Cornwall of William Haslam had already been extensively awakened to the truth of the gospel and had known much of the power of true religion before those revivals of 1848-51 and 1851-54 in which Billy Bray was involved.

'You seem a very temperate people here, and in comfortable circumstance,' commented Cardinal Newman on a walking tour in Cornwall to a miner whom he met on the way. 'How do you account for it?' The miner, slowly lifting his hat, made answer: 'There came a man among us once. His name was John Wesley.'[2]

John Wesley first visited Cornwall in 1743 and from then on he and his brother Charles went there almost every year preaching in what became one of the most fruitful fields of their evangelistic labours. John Wesley preached frequently to 'immense multitudes' in Gwenapp Pit, a disused open copper mine, from 1762 onwards. The Pit was a natural hollow of land far larger than the neatly laid out arena which can be seen today three miles south-east of Redruth. The Wesleys and their preachers succeeded in establishing throughout Cornwall a number of Methodist societies, but many of them were quite small.

Outstanding conversions

Some notable conversions had taken place during Wesley's time and many of these were marked by great conviction of sin. When *William Carvosso* heard Thomas Hanson preach at Newlyn, in 1771, he wrote, 'I had such a sight of the damning nature of sin,

John Wesley, preaching at Gwennap Pit

and of what I had done against God, that I was afraid the earth would open and swallow me up.'[3] His spiritual conflict lasted for days, until 'Christ appeared within, and God pardoned all my sins, and set my soul at liberty. The Spirit itself now bore witness with my spirit that I was a child of God. This was about nine o'clock at night, May 7th, 1771, and never shall I forget that happy hour.'[4]

Richard Trewavas, of Mousehole, a King's Pilot, paced the deck of his ship in the midst of a storm, mourning his sins, and came to see that 'without an interest in the Redeemer's merits I must be eternally undone, and that this could only be obtained by faith in Christ.'[5] After six months' of spiritual travail he found peace at a Methodist prayer meeting and joined the society.

Solomon Burall wandered for days among the mine workings around Tuckingmill in spiritual distress, until his cries to God brought a crowd of miners running to his assistance thinking he was in physical pain.[6]

The Methodist Society stewards did not know what to make of *John Chapman's* account of his conversion. His work was that of a roadman. He had been troubled about his spiritual state for some time, but was fearful of attending the local chapel. One day as he was taking his lunch break with his bread and cheese, sitting under a hedge by the roadside, a robin settled nearby. He held out a crumb in his hand to entice the robin to take it, and said, 'Come, come, come to me: you don't know how much good I can do for 'ee.' The next moment he looked up, and in his account he said, 'There was the Lord Jesus right in front of me, holding out his hand with nail prints in it. And 'twas like as if he said them words over again — "Come, come, come to me: you don't know how much good I can do you."' And so he passed from death to life.[7] His subsequent godly life convinced everyone of the genuineness of his conversion.

Of these four converts, William Carvosso was the most significant and was later to be involved in many of the Cornish

William Carvosso
1750-1834

revivals which took place in the first thirty years of the nineteenth century. His judicious, sensitive record of these revivals, later published in 1835 by his son Benjamin Carvosso as *A Memoir of Mr William Carvosso*, has provided much of the chronology and detail found in this and the following chapter.

The Methodist Magazine contains further supporting evidence and detail. Carvosso was not a preacher nor an ordained minister. His outstanding gift was that of an exhorter and an encourager (cf. Romans 12:8), a gift or function within the church which regrettably seems to have fallen into disuse. This godly man was used in many of the revivals to exhort and counsel those calling upon God and to encourage backsliders to repent and to seek his restoring mercy. Carvosso's observations are both reliable and balanced.

The above conversions took place in the pioneering days of the Evangelical Revival. Thomas Wills of Spa Fields Chapel, London, once described as second only to George Whitefield as a preacher, had been curate at St Agnes from 1764-1778. When he undertook a preaching tour of Cornwall in June and July 1781 thousands gathered to hear him preach in the open air, and much solemnity attended the occasions. A few Independent chapels came into being as the result of his labours.

Years of exceptional growth

Throughout these years the Methodist societies in Cornwall grew steadily and by 1790 there were 4,000 members connected to them. But from the mid-1790s to 1820 there was a remarkable increase as membership rose from 4,000 to 14,000; and in the period from 1820-1840 membership increased again from 14,000 to 26,000.

This growth can be illustrated by the records of the Methodist Cornish District (two thirds of Cornwall west of St Austell). In 1771 it consisted of two circuits with seven full-time preachers and 2,311 members. There were no schools, few chapels or local preachers. By 1835 the situation had been transformed. Now there were thirteen circuits; twenty-five full-time preachers; 18,122 members, and altogether 55,000 adherents attending 220 chapels in which 290 local preachers regularly preached the gospel. This transformation was effected by a series of significant revivals which began in the mid 1790s. Numbers were to increase yet further as we learn from the religious census of 1851. The population of Cornwall was then 356,641. Church attendance

Cornwall, showing where some of the revivals took place

was 174,611 (49%) of which 113,510 were Methodists (32% of the population).[8]

Before the mid 1790s there had been a marked decline, and conversions had become infrequent compared with the early days. From 1795 a degree of spiritual quickening was experienced. The people became concerned for the cause of true religion, and began to call upon God to visit them. Conversions became more frequent, and in a number of places the power of God was again in evidence. Cornwall was soon to witness the wonderful works of God in greater power and extent than ever before.

Revivals of 1799

Revival broke out in many places in Cornwall in 1799. Numerous outpourings of the Spirit in Penzance resulted in one hundred new members. At Zennor, north of Penzance, the Methodist society increased from seventeen to one hundred. Similar increases occurred in other societies within the Penzance circuit. At Walls, eighty were added in two months. Cornwall was now aflame with God. One hundred and fifty were converted in two days and nights at St Ives. In a few weeks the society there, which had numbered some one hundred and sixty for many years, increased to five hundred and fifty. The whole town of St Just was transformed when three hundred were converted in a few weeks. The Penzance circuit increased by 1100 members over a period of just three months. The Redruth circuit was also powerfully revived with some 2,500 new members being added within two months. The Truro society increased from one hundred and thirty to two hundred and eighty. At Gwennap two hundred were added and four hundred at St Agnes. These are only cold statistics, but the movements of God which lie behind them are wonderful to relate. *The Methodist Magazines* for 1799 and 1800 contain some amazing details.

'The Great Revival' of Redruth

The heavens were truly opened at Redruth in 1814 with perhaps the most astonishing revival to have taken place in Cornwall. George Smith, a Cornishman himself, described it as 'one of the most remarkable and extensive revivals of religion ever known in this or any other country.'[9] It affected the whole peninsula beyond Truro, and became known as 'The Great Revival'.

Meetings for worship had been well attended during the latter months of 1813, and in the early weeks of 1814 a growing solemnity came over the people. In early February a prayer meeting was held in a Redruth workhouse at which eight found peace with God. The following night, at another prayer meeting, many more were seized with conviction of sin, and after much agony of soul and importunate prayer they sought and found refuge in Christ. After this the spiritual interest and alarm became widespread, and in the course of the following week many hundreds in Redruth and the surrounding area were brought under deep spiritual concern. Men and women and young people who had lived godless lives were brought under great distress of soul and called upon God for mercy. Hundreds began to testify with great assurance that God had visited them and given them forgiveness of sins through the merits of Jesus Christ.

Benjamin Carvosso, son of William Carvosso, whose *Memoir* is a mine of information about this and subsequent revivals in Cornwall, describes how he witnessed it:

> About a week after the extraordinary work commenced, the rumour of it drew me to the scene, and I spent the greater part of one night with the people in the chapel. The pungency of the 'penitential pain', the extent of the distress, the fervour of devotion, the number of happy young converts whose countenances were beaming with joy, far exceeded anything of

the kind I have yet witnessed. The heavenly flame was soon carried to the various societies in the Circuit; and in those different places, similar scenes were presented to the wondering beholders.[10]

At nearby Tuckingmill the effect of the revival was astonishing. A family gathering for prayer on a Saturday morning began to attract neighbours and friends, and so many crowded into the house that after several hours the meeting had to be transferred to the chapel for lack of space. The prayer meeting continued on into Sunday with the penitents becoming so preoccupied with entreating God that the preacher appointed for the evening service could not be heard. Instead he spent the rest of the night comforting the distressed in spirit. The outpouring of divine power was so great that all attempts to bring the meeting to a close failed. It continued day and night without intermission until the following Friday morning with people coming and going all the time. The following is a description of the meeting:

> ...hundreds were crying for mercy at once. Some remained in great distress of soul for one hour, some for two, some six, some nine, twelve and some for fifteen hours before the Lord spoke peace to their souls — then they would rise, extend their arms, and proclaim the wonderful works of God, with such energy, that bystanders would be struck in a moment, and fall to the ground and roar for the disquietude of their souls.[11]

Amazingly, two thousand were converted within the first week of the revival. In a period of only a few weeks from the beginning of the revival in Redruth an estimated five to six thousand people were gathered out of the ungodly world into the kingdom of God. People of all types and social classes were converted and added to the Methodist societies. The fruits of righteousness soon appeared in the lives of many who before that time had led immoral and degraded lives. All the neighbouring circuits felt the impact of 'The Great Revival' of Redruth. God had visited his people.

The results of the awakening were undeniable. The Methodist circuits of Redruth, Truro, St Austell, Bodmin, Penzance and Helston had a total membership of 9,405 in 1813. A year later their membership was 14,616. A 55% increase had taken place within a period of five months. George Blencowe, writing in 1859 (forty-five years later), comments:

> And the results of this Divine influence have been as permanent as they were extensive and glorious. The writer has visited many mature Christian people, in old age and in affliction, who ascribe their conversion to that revival; and have shown by a long consistent life that they did not receive the grace of God in vain. [12]

The Wesleyan Chapel opened in Redruth in 1826
following the Great Revival of 1814

When one considers how spontaneous was this work of God, how totally unexpected, how powerfully effective in renewing the lives of ungodly men and women, how contagious in its influences, how lasting in its effects, and how fruitful in the multitude of souls so sovereignly converted within so brief a period of time, one sees the need of such awakenings in the life of our churches. The lesson of this revival, as of all revivals, is that the church's primary response in a day of spiritual decline should be to offer unceasing prayer to God that he might visit his people once more.

Some respond by suggesting that those who think in this way believe in doing nothing for the salvation of the lost. The implication that praying for God to visit his people is doing nothing borders on unbelief and reflects upon the low spirituality of those who make such a charge. No activity is more vital, more calculated to lead to the conversion of sinners, to restore power and effectiveness to the church and lead to the prosperity of gospel preaching, than the holy work of importunate prayer.

When God is pleased to hear the prayers of the godly, the regular channels of the life of our churches will be filled with streams of living waters, which will break the normal bounds, and stream forth from the church to satisfy the souls of needy men and women now living in ignorance of God.

Porthleven, Breage and Ponsanooth: 1817

Unusual things were also happening elsewhere in Cornwall. 'The Great Revival' of 1814 had affected other places such as Porthleven, Breage and Ponsanooth. In 1817 the Spirit had been poured out in these towns, as also in the Liskeard (early 1816) and Bodmin (1816/17) circuits, and in Sticker (Stuker) in November 1817.

Cambourne and Tuckingmill: 1821-2

Seven years after 'The Great Revival' of Redruth in 1814, which had so extensively affected the Methodist societies in that whole area of Cornwall, a further powerful quickening occurred in October 1821 at Cambourne and Tuckingmill — just three miles from Redruth.

The noteworthy conversion of two young men who were brothers was the divine match which lit the fire. In his *Memoir* William Carvosso describes what happened next:

> Soon the prayer-meetings began to increase, and the Lord poured out the Spirit of grace and supplication upon the people. At one of these meetings one evening I gave out that beautiful and favourite hymn:
>
> Thou hidden source of calm repose,
> Thou all-sufficient Love Divine...
>
> and then gave a short exhortation upon it. From the striking language of this hymn, I endeavoured to show what Christ is to the believer. While speaking, such views of the adorable Jesus were given me as I think will never be erased from my mind in time or eternity.[13]

Such visitations became the experience of many, so that Carvosso refers to one meeting when 'They felt so much of the overwhelming power of grace, that it was some time before they had bodily strength sufficient to walk home.'[14] We have already noted that in Nottingham in 1799 a sense of the glory of God had the same enervating effect on some of the people.[15] This should not surprise us, nor should it alarm us. What should concern us is that it happens so infrequently. What these people came to know was, surely, the burden of Paul's prayer for the

Ephesian believers, that they 'may be able to comprehend with all the saints what is the width and length and depth and height — to know the love of Christ which passes knowledge; that you may be filled with all the fulness of God' (Ephesians 3:18-19). It ought not to surprise us that it should empty a man of enough bodily strength to walk home on account of the sheer glory of it. Such was its effect on these Cornish believers.

Kehelland: 1822

The revival spread and during April and May 1822 it broke out in Kehelland, a mile and a half north-west of Cambourne. Carvosso describes how:

> Several of the Cambourne friends made an appointment to go to Kehelland, to hold a prayer-meeting. The news of our coming excited some curiosity among the people, so that the house was crowded within and without. The power of God descended, and many sinners were pricked in the heart: this was the drop before the shower. The Lord began a gracious work among them, and some of the most wicked and notorious sinners in the neighbourhood were awakened. Trejuthan, a spot which had remained barren and unfruitful for a number of years, now became the garden of the Lord. For some days the cloud of mercy hung over it; and so plentifully poured its precious contents on the dry ground that the deep concern for the salvation of their souls seemed to draw off the people's attention from every other object.[16]

William Carvosso relates several individual cases of conversion and of the sovereign manner in which God dealt with their souls. The characteristics of the revival bear all the evidence of a true and powerful and effectual working of the Spirit of God, as demonstrated in the following account:

> I took tea one evening at Brother Smith's: just before we were going to unite in prayer one who was a stranger to me entered the room; I had no sooner opened my mouth in prayer, than he was deeply awakened, and roared for the disquietude[17] of his soul. I think I never saw a man in my life whose anguish of spirit was greater. He was a backslider, and saw and felt his unfaithfulness and ingratitude. After a severe struggle he obtained mercy, and joyfully testified that God had pardoned all his sins.[18]

What had been happening in and around Kehelland at that time had also been taking place throughout the whole land. 1820-21 were years of a general quickening within the churches. In the year 1822 when the Kehelland revival broke out, twelve thousand members were added to the Wesleyan Methodist churches.[19]

Contemporary accounts refer to 'the power of God descending among us as a mighty rushing wind' and of 'a very gracious visitation from above.' In those days believers did not divorce evangelism from revival in their thinking. Like Jonathan Edwards they prayed for divine visitations in order to effect a spread of the gospel. They took far more seriously than we do the vital need for the sovereign activity of God within the life of the churches. The people held a true view of revival, such as had been taught by Edwards, that the blessing of God comes down from heaven and is not worked up by man. This encouraged them to look for and to pray for special visitations of God to his people, a coming down from heaven to earth of the divine influences of the Spirit. By this the whole level of the spiritual life among the people of God would be raised and astonishing works of God would take place leading to many remarkable conversions and a general public awareness of the holiness and power of God.

Men of Reformed views today can ill afford to be over-critical of these Wesleyans of two hundred years ago, whose views of spiritual life within the church allowed a far greater place for the sovereign interventions of God than we do in our day. In some respects their evangelicalism was inconsistent with biblical doctrine; an example of this was their teaching that sanctification can be received in answer to fervent prayer as an experience subsequent to conversion instead of by a growth in grace. We do not question, however, the reality of the spiritual experiences they knew following such times of prayer, only their interpretation of them. But in practice they took far more seriously than we do the imperative need for the sovereign activity of God within the life of the churches. We give lip-service to it, but they *acted* upon it. They held the view that spiritual soundness within a gospel church is not just dependent upon a faithful ministry of the Word, but also requires direct operations of the Spirit of God upon the souls of the people.

They did not hold a mystical view of revival — as is quite common today — a strange indefinable 'something' for which we must wait. Rather, they had a more biblical view of the activity of the Holy Spirit. They believed that in all the work of God constant supplies of the Spirit of God were essential.

6

THE CORNISH REVIVALS OF 1823-1840

Constantine, 1823; Ponsanooth, 1824

In November 1823 a revival broke out in Constantine (five miles south-west of Falmouth). Many ungodly men and women were awakened and converted. William Carvosso, who was in Constantine when the revival started, relates that whilst there he received news of a further work, begun this time in his own town of Ponsanooth, situated between Falmouth and Redruth. He wrote:

> Hearing that God had very wonderfully visited Ponsanooth, I hastened thither, and found some of the distressed souls in the chapel, who had been there several days and nights struggling in prayer, and crying for mercy. At Mr Lovey's factory the Spirit of conviction was operating so powerfully, that many who had been triflers were falling down on their knees to pray in the midst of their work. Indeed, for many days little else was done but attending to those who were deeply agonising with God for their soul's salvation.

Multitudes were the subjects of a gracious change: the exact number I cannot say, but upwards of a hundred gave their names to meet in class. But not only at Ponsanooth has this glorious work broken out: it has gone forth into all the societies and congregations round about to a great extent. Thousands are said to be awakened. How many, in consequence of this shaking among the dry bones, will find their way to heaven, O Lord, thou knowest. These are fair blossoms: and in due season it will appear who will bring forth fruit unto perfection. May God deal gently with them, and show them mercy unto eternal life. Amen and amen.[1]

This revival became general, spreading throughout all the surrounding countryside, affecting many villages and towns. Thousands were awakened and brought to faith in Christ. Years later, most of those who testified to having received forgiveness of sins in this revival were found continuing steadfastly in the faith.

Other revivals had been breaking out elsewhere. The St Austell Circuit experienced a quickening in 1826. The Rev. W. Lawry described it as 'a steady, deep and awful feeling after God.'[2] Sticker and Charlestown were also deeply affected in this work of God.

Mevagissey revival: 1827

Part of the same general awakening, yet distinct from it in its origin, was the revival at Mevagissey in the spring of 1827. It began with the striking conversion of a woman of eighty years of age. She had attended class meetings for thirty years, and yet was only formally religious. She was warned of the danger of resting satisfied without the evidence of having been accepted in the Son of God, and of the impossibility of getting to heaven without being born again. Pricked in her heart, she fell upon her knees, and began to cry to God for mercy. 'Lord, save me from dropping into hell,' she cried. Her cries became loud and vehement, and soon the Lord mercifully visited her soul and gave her the 'knowledge of salvation ... by the remission of sins.' We read:

> Her face shone as it had been the face of an angel, and she went round the room, clapping with her hands, and shouting the praises of God; apparently with all the activity of a girl of fifteen, although she was then fourscore.[3]

We need to remember that the work of grace does not obliterate personal or regional characteristics.

This conversion was followed by prayer-meetings held every night for seven weeks. In Cornwall unconverted people frequently attended the prayer-meetings and many were saved

Mevagissey Cliff Street and harbour

at such meetings. Some amazing conversions took place in Mevagissey at this time. The convicting work of the Spirit of God was so great that on occasions the cries of the people calling upon God for mercy within their homes could be heard by those walking along the streets. Carvosso records that, 'Upwards of one hundred and fifty were brought to the Lord, besides a great number of children.'[4] He was much used by God in this revival, counselling troubled souls for which he was unusually gifted. He comments in his journal:

> The eight weeks I was with them, I could seldom get to bed before one in the morning: and sometimes I was called again before breakfast to visit persons in great distress. But the Lord gave me strength according to my day.[5]

He was seventy-seven years of age at the time.

People of all ages were brought to salvation. Among the older ones were two brothers in their sixties. Carvosso describes the conversion of the elder in the following words:

> The wife of the elder brother had long been a pious member of the society; he was her persecutor, and seldom or never attended the house of God. The Lord found him out in his dwelling; and, hearing that he had begun to pray, I was requested to visit him. I had not long conversed with him before he was more deeply awakened, and began to cry aloud for mercy. After praying with him I left him. In the evening I called on him again; and while I was pointing him to the Lamb of God that taketh away the sin of the world, God revealed His mercy to his soul, and he cried out, 'My burden is gone, the Lord has pardoned all my sins: glory, glory be to His Name!' I saw him several times afterwards and found his confidence unshaken; and, what is rather remarkable, he told me he could never sing before, but now he was singing and praising God all day long.[6]

The Cornish revivals of 1823-1840

Mylor Bridge and Flushing area: 1827 and 1833

During times of revival particular towns or areas are sometimes resistant to the work of the Spirit. In the days of our Lord there were towns where he could not do any mighty work on account of their unbelief (Matthew 13:58); and so it was in Cornwall. The Mylor Bridge and Flushing area, just north of Falmouth, had long resisted the gospel; but in 1827, the year of the Mevagissey revival, it yielded. The exalted Son of God commanded his blessing, and the Spirit of the Lord was poured out upon the people. Many were awakened and converted, including the grandson of William Carvosso. The account of his conversion by his grandfather is worth noting:

> My dear grandson, William Rundle, so recently brought to God, and so hopeful in the church, has been snatched away from us by the hand of death. He was ill only a very short time; but glory be to God, he died in sure and certain hope of a glorious resurrection to eternal life. How merciful are the dispensations of God! His conversion took place about six weeks before his removal from hence. He did not long groan under the burden of guilt, and his evidence of pardon and adoption was very clear. At a prayer-meeting two or three weeks before his death, he received an overwhelming manifestation of the Spirit, in which every doubt and fear was utterly put to flight. He attended his class a few days before his death, and seemed to be filled with unspeakable joy: 'My soul', he said, 'is like a ship in full sail, on the boundless ocean of redeeming love.' His death was occasioned by the rupture of a blood vessel. In all the conflict, he was perfectly tranquil and serene; fear was not permitted to come near him. This was the more striking, because, in every little indisposition before, he was much alarmed and distressed at the thought of death. But now he seemed at once ready-winged for the flight. To his father, who had fondly hoped that

he would be the help and comfort of his advancing years, he said, 'Father, you can do very well without me; and I would rather die than live.' The Lord whom he had so heartily chosen for his portion in the vigour of health, was now his abundant support in the struggle of pain and death. Just before he expired, he said to me, 'I used to be struck with terror at the thought of dying, but now I can meet death with a smile.' He died in his nineteenth year.[7]

This one example of the powerful results of the revival at Mylor Bridge in 1827 demonstrates the degree of faith, assurance and hope given to believers at such times. It helps us to understand what John Wesley meant when he declared, 'Our people die well!' Some gave outstanding testimony face to face with 'the last enemy'.

The favour of God continued towards the people in the Mylor Bridge and Flushing area. Six years later, in a letter written at the end of 1833, William Carvosso comments: 'I suppose you have heard how the Lord is pouring out his Spirit at Mylor Bridge. Such a sight, at this place, I have never seen before.'[8] Prayer meetings were held night after night for months on end. The glory and power of the revival in 1833 exceeded that of 1827.

These things should encourage us, for who knows whether God may yet work again in our nation, such a work as will exceed in glory all that has formerly preceded it. One often hears it said that we cannot expect frequent revivals and that therefore it is not the will of God for his church. The statement is made, one suspects, because such an experience has never been part of the history of the church for a very long time — not, at least, in the Western world. In addition, as we look back on the recent history of revivals in Britain, it would seem that events of this nature can only be expected very occasionally. For instance, the time span between the 1859 revival in Ireland and Wales, the Welsh revival of 1904-5, the Lowestoft/Fraserburgh/Peterhead revival of 1921 and the Lewis revival of 1949-53 seems to support such a view. It is this consideration which gives rise to the notion that revivals are so abnormal that we need not give too much attention to them.[9] The normal testimony of the church, we are told, is to be advanced by the activity of evangelism as distinct from revival, and that the churches cannot be expected to depend upon revivals. This emphasis raises serious questions and inevitably produces the mentality that an interest in revival and special prayer for revival is a luxury in which believers can ill afford to indulge. Instead they ought to be getting on with the very practical task of evangelizing the lost.

The churches of the New Testament were generally in a condition of revival over a period of more than thirty years. The New Testament assumes such a condition and the book of Acts describes it, whilst the epistles were mainly written to counteract influences which threatened to lead the churches away from that high level of spiritual life and experience. The Evangelical Revival in the eighteenth century was also continuous in nature, with visitation upon visitation in different towns and areas over a period of forty years or so. This too, as we have seen, was the character of the work of God in Cornwall in the early nineteenth century.

The necessity of revivals

Important lessons arise from the above observations. The periods in the history of the church when the ungodly are effectively gathered in and the world is influenced to any marked degree are days of revival. Apart from revivals and their continuing repercussions in the years which immediately follow, the church is usually found in a state of spiritual decline. It was this awareness which focused the attention of our spiritual fathers upon the absolute necessity of revivals. When they considered the lack of conversions, their minds turned not to the subject of evangelism but to the need of God's intervention. This is not to suggest that they had no interest in evangelism, but rather that they knew that their preaching and witnessing would bear little fruit unless God was pleased to give them spiritual power. The only really effective evangelism is that which arises out of a divine visitation. After all, there is no such thing as a conversion apart from this. The issue is not a question of evangelism *or* revival, nor is it one of evangelism *and* revival; it is that effective evangelism must arise out of a movement of the Spirit.

Solomon Stoddard, the grandfather and predecessor of Jonathan Edwards in Northampton in New England, was pastor of the church for sixty years, during which time he faithfully preached the gospel consistently; but looking back over those years, he was able to identify 'five harvests' when God came in power and called the lost into his kingdom. He was a Calvinist, and the Wesleyans in Cornwall were Arminians; but what they shared in common was the view that since conversion is a work of God, it will only take place when God is pleased to act. Therefore, they believed in, prayed for, and looked for such movements of God's Spirit. We must do likewise.

In this period of Cornish religious history, revivals were constant occurrences. Beginning with 'The Great Revival' of 1814 in Redruth, and continuing for a period of some thirty or forty years, the story is one of many revivals, here and there, in this village or then in another, sometimes the same place was visited more than once, with but a few years intervening. We tend to think that revivals can only be rare events, but in Cornwall at this time, the life of the churches was akin to that in the Acts of the Apostles.

Awakenings in Mousehole: 1818 and 1828

One of the most amazing works of God ever to take place in Cornwall was at Mousehole, the scene of the tragic Penlee lifeboat disaster of December 1981. Today Mousehole is a godless and materialistic community, but the massive Methodist chapel there gives a hint of the mighty acts of God which so powerfully blessed the lives of its inhabitants in former days.

William Carvosso, whose informative *Memoir* is the main source for much of the information that follows, was born in Mousehole in 1750 and was converted in May 1771.[10] The Methodist society at Mousehole at that time had barely twenty members. Twelve years later, in 1783, the first chapel was built, and much enlarged in 1813 to accommodate increasing congregations. But the first great movement of God's Spirit occurred in February 1818. Carvosso records something of what he witnessed there at that time:

> I proceeded to Mousehole where I rejoiced to see the mighty works of God displayed in convincing and converting sinners … In my usual way, I went preaching from house to house, and I believe God never blessed my feeble effort more than at that time. In one house I found a poor penitent to whose broken heart the Lord revealed his pardoning mercy. We fell on our knees, to give glory to God for what he had done. And now a brother of her who had been the subject of the happy change, being present, fell on the floor, and cried for mercy in an astonishing manner; and, before I left the house, the Lord also set his soul at liberty. In another house, while relating this circumstance, the arrow of truth reached the heart of a poor backslider, and she trembled as in the presence of God. The next morning I found her weeping for her ingratitude and now made willing to return to her offended God … There was a gracious work among the children in the Sunday School. None but those who have witnessed such a revival can form any idea of it. Some of them seemed as deeply convinced of sin as if they had been forty years of age; and after they had found peace, could give as clear an account of the work of grace in their minds as if they had been in the good way seven years.[11]

Where today in our nation can we find sinners crying out to God for mercy; and where do we find men and women physically trembling before a holy God; and where can we discover children of tender years under such conviction of sin that nothing but a powerful work of grace — of which afterwards they are able to give a clear account — can bring their souls peace?

Ten years later, in 1828, Mousehole was visited again in an even more powerful work of God. The floodtide of 1818 had ebbed a little, and Satan had been at work sowing discord within the church, so that some believers had become estranged from one another. They were brought to repent before God over this disunity. This was followed by earnest prayer being offered to God to revive his work among them. The prayer meetings which had begun in private homes increased so rapidly that they had to be transferred to the chapel. Soon hundreds were attending

Mousehole Wesleyan Church

Plaque on church reads: 'Built 1784, enlarged 1814; rebuilt 1833, renovated 1905' the prayer meetings, and the whole town was filled with a sense of the presence of God.

News of the divine visitation quickly spread. Many travelled to Mousehole from a distance to witness the mighty work of God. This fact alone demonstrates the genuine character of these movements as sovereign acts of God in true revival; even in those days, though they occurred with such frequency, they were regarded as phenomenal. They were not worked up or produced in any way by men. They were the wonderful works of God to which people were drawn as to a divine spectacle.

So powerful was the revival in Mousehole that within a short time the movement spread to other towns and villages. Two hundred people in Mousehole alone, out of a population of just one thousand, were added to the Methodist society. The character of the whole town was transformed as those of a blasphemous and immoral life were saved from their wickedness and brought into the joys of salvation. The main work was done over a period of four months. To obtain some idea of the extraordinary impact and power of this work of God, one only has to imagine the conversion of one fifth of the population of one's own home town within a period of just sixteen weeks.

William Carvosso gives his usual balanced summary of what took place:

The prayer meetings were crowded by hundreds of attendants, and all the enquiry was, 'What must I do to be saved?' Some of the most hardened sinners were cut to the heart and cried aloud for mercy; and the work of God went forward with mighty power. This extraordinary visitation from above continued four months; and 'the revival at Mousehole' resounded far and near. Vast numbers, moved by different motives, came from a distance of many miles to see the wonderful works of God; and not a few of the strangers who came from curiosity were converted in the chapel at Mousehole... Thus the heavenly fire was carried to different villages and societies in the Circuit; and the thanksgiving of many redounded to the glory of God. This revival was carried on in the best order I have ever seen one in my life... Mousehole now appears like a new town.[12]

He then refers to a decline in worldly conversation, a loss of interest in traditional amusements and recreations, a quickened interest in the Lord's day, and how even the children became more engaged in serious pursuits. He further comments:

These little facts serve to show what a universal seriousness pervaded all ages and classes... The wonders of the Lord, daily displayed in the conviction and conversion of sinners, seemed to engross nearly the whole conversation of the place. During the four months that I was with them there were very few houses in Mousehole that I did not visit from religious motives; and very few men, women or children with whom I did not converse on the necessity of preparing to meet God.[13]

One of Carvosso's most striking observations on the revival was that 'four months appeared as only four days.'[14] Conversions continued frequently in Mousehole right up to and through 1831 and 1832, when an extraordinary work of God took place in almost every Methodist society throughout the extensive Penzance circuit. In that year, and the few following years, powerful revivals broke out again in many different parts of Cornwall.

Cambourne circuit: 1831

Following the Ponsanooth revival of 1824,[15] the town was again visited by another powerful revival in 1831. Upwards of fifty were added to the church. This was a year of general revival in Cornwall. In a letter written to Jabez Bunting, dated 26 March

1831, Henry Davies, superintendent minister of the Cambourne circuit from 1830 to 1832, describes the effect of the awakening:

> ...In the course of the past quarter it has pleased the great Head of the Church to favour this circuit with a most extensive effusion of divine influence. Every place in the circuit, small and large, has participated in it... The great work commenced on the 16th of January and continued about eight weeks. In some places, it is going on still. Our society being previously upwards of 1400 we have thus given tickets and notes to more than 2750 persons... It appears to me, we ought to think of applying to the next Conference for an additional preacher.[16]

Redruth: 1839

William Dale, an influential layman of Truro, in a letter to Jabez Bunting dated 12 July 1839 wrote, 'You have no doubt heard of the glorious revival of religion that has taken place in several of the Cornish circuits, that upwards of five thousand have been added to the Societies in the District since the last Conference.'[17] And in a letter from John Hobson, superintendent minister of the Redruth circuit, dated 27 January 1840, addressed to Bunting, we read:

> ...Methodism is rising in the Town; and in one of our country places (Wheal Rose) about 60 persons have during the last fortnight been converted to God. In one house where a number of penitents had met in the day time, to unite in prayer for mercy and salvation, a farmer's wife was crying for mercy; and her husband, who was ploughing with a yoke of oxen, on hearing his good wife praying for mercy, left the oxen to go and pray with his wife and the other penitents; and he remained nearly *six hours* in the meeting; and when his good wife had found peace, the good man returned to the field and found the

oxen had remained *all that time exactly in the place* in which he had left them!

We have had many interesting incidents of a similar character; and we hope the good Lord will yet by thousands convert sinners and join them to himself and his people...[18]

Cornwall today

The Cornwall of the present day is a very different place from what it was in the past. Most of the tin and copper mines have now been closed down and this has shifted the concentration of the population from the inland areas to the coastal towns and villages, with tourism as the main industry. Many have moved into Cornwall from other parts of the country. Some towns have been almost taken over by certain interest groups. St Ives, with its numerous resident artists and over forty craft shops, is a notable example of this. Modern Cornwall is very unlike the Cornwall of Carvosso's day.

But one sad feature of the changes which have come to the area is the decline of vital New Testament Christianity. This has been taking place over the past hundred years. Cornwall used to be a stronghold of Methodism, but with the rise of theological liberalism within the denomination and a rejection of biblical authority Methodism has lost its spiritual power and influence. Nowhere has this been more evident than in Cornwall where in the sixties and seventies of the last century Methodist chapels were being closed at the rate of one each week.

Apart from its name, modern Methodism has little in common with the Methodism described in this book. It is virtually a different religion. And in our judgement its rejection of its past heritage and biblical convictions is responsible for Methodism's serious decline and present ineffectiveness. What Cornwall needs is a resurgence of the old spiritual powers.

7

HOW THE WESLEYANS REGARDED
THE WORK OF GOD

Some Christians are only interested in those acts of God which have taken place among believers of their own particular denomination or theological persuasion. But since all true religion is a work of God we ought to be interested in it wherever he chooses to work; otherwise we must ask whether we are more interested in the activity of 'our men' than in the works of God. This is not to suggest that the truth is unimportant, it is all-important; but when other believers are committed to the primary truths of Scripture, it is unworthy of us to dismiss the activity of God among those who differ from us on secondary issues as if such divine work were of no consequence.

We may not agree with all the theology of the Wesleyan Methodists in the period under review, nor with some of their interpretations of their own experiences — though of a genuine spiritual character — yet these revivals were clearly God's work. This was how *they* understood it. In the minutes of the Wesleyan Methodist Conference for the year 1821, when God was adding thousands to their churches, the following resolution was subscribed by the preachers:

> We again resolve, after the example of our venerable fathers in
> the gospel, with all plainness and zeal, to preach a free, present,
> and full salvation from sin; a salvation flowing from the mere
> grace of God, through the redemption which is in Christ Jesus,
> apprehended by the simple exercise of faith, and indispensably
> preparatory to a course of practical holiness. And in this great
> work, our only reliance for success is upon the grace of the Holy
> Spirit; by whose inspiration alone it is, that the Gospel, in any
> instance, is rendered the 'power of God unto salvation'.

That last sentence shows how little confidence these men
placed in 'the arm of the flesh'; how little concern they had for
technique or method; and how far from their thinking was any
idea that to reach the lost some special 'outreach' or 'mission'
was needed. As we have already observed, in the second half
of the nineteenth century, revivals in Cornwall began to be
overlapped by what many regarded as 'new-fangled' special
missions. 'Instead of praying that revivals might come', said
a Bible Christian leader in 1889, 'they hired people to get up
revivals.'[1]

Thomas Cook was an example of one who started to use the
new methods. At Cambourne in 1888 he introduced the novelty
of the inquiry room. This caused many of the local leaders to
shake their heads in disapproval. Despite this, Cook experienced
genuine revival during a number of his missions somewhat to
his own surprise.[2]

Up until the 1870s the Wesleyans, in the main, believed in
reaching the lost through the witness of their own members,
and they believed that their preachers should be continually
declaring the gospel. In addition they regarded conversion as a
sovereign work of God, without which no human explanation of
the gospel or persuasion was of any avail.

There is much to learn from these accounts. The Wesleyans
were Arminian in their theology, but their Arminianism was

not the semi-Pelagianism which prevailed among twentieth-century evangelicals until the 1960s when Reformed emphases were restored to some extent. Their view of conversion and of the work of God was essentially more biblical than that held by many among us today. This was particularly so in the following respects.

Their understanding of conversion

They thought of conversion as God coming to a man with saving power — and of God declaring peace to his heart by the Holy Spirit. And their view of what a person needs to do to be saved from their sins followed from this. Men and women must call upon God for mercy through Jesus Christ — and that involves both repentance and faith. The mere act of calling was not regarded as salvation — God had to act, God had to come. There was no talk about 'commitment'; no mention of 'decision'. Obviously they were not against commitment or resolution in the Christian life, but it had little place in their view of conversion.

They made a valid distinction between a sinner being awakened, and true conversion. When confronted by seekers desiring to be saved from their sins, they did not imagine that some simple gospel ABC was all that was required, or that they had the ability in any way to deliver a sinner from the agony of his conviction and bring him to the assurance of sins forgiven. They preached the gospel and enforced it with frequent exhortations, but having done this they left the seeker in the hands of God. The reason for such an approach is clear from the revival records. They regarded salvation not primarily as the sinner coming to God in response to the gospel, but as God coming to the sinner through the gospel in the power of the Holy Spirit (cf. 1 Thessalonians 1:5-6). Nor did they believe that God could be made to come. For this reason they left those convicted of their sins crying out for mercy, and urged them to cry and cry again until God bore witness by his Spirit that they had become his children.

This is not the emphasis which prevails today. Assent to evangelical truth and affirmation of a sincere desire to be committed to Christ is all that is usually expected or required. But all this is possible quite apart from any work of God in the soul. Today we have lost that necessary and biblical emphasis upon salvation as primarily an act of God. There are a number of reasons for this. One reason is an increasing neglect of the biblical terminology 'to be *saved*,' a concept which underlines the helplessness of man and the need of a direct intervention by God in salvation. Another is the idea that men and women can be saved whenever they want to be, irrespective of the attitude of God towards them.

The Methodists in Cornwall did not make that presumption. Their view of salvation was entirely supernaturalistic. God alone could save a sinner, and he would do so when it pleased him and only then. This did not lead them to a position of passivity — the idea that man can do nothing and must just wait for God to act. They urged men and women to believe the gospel; but they went beyond this, and urged sinners to seek the Lord and to call upon him for mercy. They knew that under true conviction, and as evidence of true repentance, sinners would earnestly and sincerely do this and that God would hear their cry.

These Wesleyans did not take the mercy of God for granted; it had to be sought, but the activity of seeking was no final evidence of salvation. God had to respond to the seeking sinner, and when he did so he would speak peace directly to the soul. Man was seen as totally dependent upon God for salvation; and this is where these Wesleyans brought seeking souls, mentally, experimentally and emotionally. Theirs was a truer biblical emphasis than is found in most evangelical churches today.

Their understanding of the nature of true religion

Above everything else, the Cornish Wesleyans believed that true religion is a work of the living God. The supernaturalism which distinguishes the Christian faith from all other religions was at the forefront of their thinking. They expected God to visit them and deal personally and directly with their souls. This view prevailed throughout the Wesleyan Methodist societies in Cornwall in the early nineteenth century. They believed in a God who takes the initiative; and so they were not primarily concerned with their own activities, but in the doings of God among them. They knew that the prosperity of their churches and their own blessedness depended upon God coming down and visiting them. They were not familiar with the teaching of Jonathan Edwards upon the subject of divine visitations, though he had influenced the Wesley brothers and the early pioneers of English as well as Welsh Methodism. The people learnt from their reading of the Bible to expect such visitations, and their experience of the power of God coming down upon them confirmed their expectations.

These simple, believing men and women looked for the wonderful works of God among them. They believed that unless God worked they were powerless to achieve anything in his name. This explains why they prayed so much and with such great earnestness. There is no evidence at this time that they arranged special evangelistic missions to reach the lost. Such missions were first introduced in England by High Churchmen. These Wesleyans looked for the power of God coming upon the regular class meetings, prayer meetings and services, and when this happened the lost were saved, either in those meetings or subsequently, through the revived testimony of the members. When God visited them all their meetings became special. Prayer meetings and services took place which had not been planned. Sinners began to seek the Lord without the help of any novel contrivances introduced by the churches; and church members expressed their experience of the quickening power of God in demanding prayer meeting after prayer meeting.

The desires and aspirations of these Methodist believers were easily satisfied. They did not crave entertainment or novelty, but were hungry for God. And when God gave them the bread of heaven they were satisfied. In their zeal they witnessed spontaneously to the saving power of Jesus Christ, and visited the homes of their neighbours with warm desire to see them enter into the same spiritual blessings. There was little need to publish the testimonies of these believers. They were their own publicity. They freely testified of the forgiveness of sins and of having received the inner witness of the Spirit (Romans 8:16; Galatians 4:6). Their evangelism was no more a formal and self-conscious activity than was that of the early Christians. It was the spontaneous expression of their faith and not some 'outreach' organized by the churches.

Equally strange to them would have been the modern talk about the need of 'renewal' within the churches. Renewal, as they understood it, is what takes place when men and women are born again by God's Spirit, and the church is the company of renewed men and women. The Methodist societies in Cornwall in the early nineteenth century experienced times of spiritual declension and backsliding, but at such times the believers looked for revival, not renewal. They prayed for a quickening of the life they already had. They sought the heavenly influences of the Spirit of God to fan afresh the glowing embers of their spiritual life.

This belief in the necessity of revivals for the progress of true religion led in practice to a far greater emphasis upon the sovereignty of God than is evident in our modern evangelical churches. This serves to prove that doctrine has to be experienced before it really takes hold of men and women, and that is what had happened to these Methodists.

There has been a tendency in Reformed and evangelical circles to confine God to the pages of the Bible, as though to suggest that because God has spoken and made himself known through the Scriptures he no longer deals directly and personally with men. This can easily lead to what Walter Cradock, the Puritan, once described as 'a frozen knowledge of God.' The knowledge may be correct, yet lacking any personal acquaintance with God.

It is not true that God equals the Bible, as though he has no independent existence. The Bible as the word of God has been given in the past by inspiration of the Holy Spirit. But in the present, individuals and especially churches are in need of a continuing activity of God to make the truth of God's word effective for the salvation of the lost and the sanctifying of believers. This is why Jesus prayed the Father to sanctify the disciples through his word of truth (John 17:17). There has to be an activity of God in addition to the word (1 Thessalonians 1:5-6; 2 Thessalonians 2:13).

But so often today, it is as though we concede no such independence to God apart from the Scripture. We are in danger of making God remote. The Bible tends to take the place of God and consequently of the Holy Spirit, and so we no longer deal with God himself as a person. We shut God up in a book. But the function of Scripture is surely to bring us into communion with the living God. We must become aware of God himself: Father, Son and Holy Spirit. The comment of Charles Hodge, the Princeton theologian, is applicable here.

> In short, the whole Bible, and especially the evangelical history and the epistles of the New Testament, represents the Holy Spirit not as a power imprisoned in the truth, but as a personal, voluntary agent acting with the truth, or without it, as He pleases. As such He has ever been regarded by the Church, and has ever exhibited Himself in His dealings with the children of God.[3]

It was this awareness of the living God which caused these Cornish Christians to seek the activity of God in revivals. They regarded revivals as necessary for the progress of true religion, and this in practice led to a far greater emphasis upon the sovereignty of God than is evident in our modern evangelical churches.

The greatest single hindrance to revival in our day is surely our failure to think in the *biblical* manner so characteristic of these humble Cornish Christians. The thought of divine visitations is so strange to us that whenever we hear of any church experiencing the blessing of God we enquire exactly how things have happened and then institutionalize it by turning it into a method. Like Charles Finney, we think of man's actions as being the key to God's action, instead of thinking biblically of God's action as being the key to man's spiritual actions.

The history of the work of God among the Methodists in Cornwall in the first forty years of the nineteenth century illustrates that the work of evangelism is generally promoted by revivals of religion. Evangelism alone cannot produce lasting results, unless it is accompanied by a movement of the Holy Spirit. We claim to believe in revivals, yet when it comes to church practice and the topic of evangelism we act as though we do not believe. We hold the doctrines of revival and evangelism in isolation, instead of seeing that they are inextricably linked together.

The promised presence and activity of Christ in the midst of his people undergirds obedience to the Great Commission (Matthew 28:18-20). The early Christians had to wait for the divine power of the Holy Spirit before witnessing to Jesus Christ (Acts 1:4-8). And when the Holy Spirit was given, and they were endued with power, they did not regard him as some sort of given 'reservoir' from which they could scoop up power whenever required. They had to maintain a personal relationship with Christ and seek fresh supplies of the Spirit's power by prayer and submission to his will (Acts 4:23-31; Philippians 1:19).

The evangelism of the early church arose out of a work of God within the souls of his people (cf. Acts 13:1-3). The Lord is always represented as taking the initiative in evangelism, and this is why it was always a spontaneous activity. The early Christians continually sought to discern the mind of God so as to act where he was acting (cp. Acts 16:6-10). Their evangelism was not contrived or highly organized. It was the spontaneous outworking of their faith and life in Jesus Christ. Roland Allen has drawn attention to the fact that it is a natural instinct in men and women to wish to share new-found joys and experiences with others:

> It is not surprising then that when Christians are scattered and feel solitary this craving for fellowship should demand an outlet, especially when the hope of the Gospel and the experience of its power is something new and wonderful. But in Christians there is more than this natural instinct. The Spirit of Christ is a Spirit who longs for, and strives after, the salvation of the souls of men, and that Spirit dwells in them. That Spirit converts the natural instinct into a longing for the conversion of others which is indeed divine in its source and character.[4]

Nowhere in the New Testament do we find further exhortations to evangelism beyond the giving of the Great Commission. This does not mean that the early church was disinterested in spreading the gospel. Far from it! Their obedience to the Great Commission had the character of spontaneity. It was the outflowing of their spiritual life and testimony to the world. For them evangelism was not a specialized interest or an irregular event, but an essential part of their daily spiritual life.

The concern of the New Testament writers is to clarify the thinking of their readers as to the true nature of the gospel and of the character of the church, and to urge believers to live holy lives. 'What we read in the New Testament is no anxious appeal to Christians to spread the Gospel,' commented Roland Allen.[5] Instead we are informed of how the gospel was spreading and the church increasing in size and influence (Acts 8:4; 16:3; 1 Thessalonians 1:8). The church in its true expression should have a magnetism and an appeal which draws needy sinners to it (cf. Isaiah 2:2-4; Micah 4:1-3; Zechariah 8:20-23). Here is the reason for the amazing growth of the church in China since the missionaries left. The believers in that land have had no opportunity to organize formal evangelism, but millions have been brought to Christ.

We need to get back to this New Testament way of thinking in terms of divine initiatives, of the acts of God, of power being poured out from on high, of spontaneous evangelism arising from quickenings and promptings of the Spirit. Without these, our labours can do but little to advance the kingdom of God in this sinning world. If we continue to think that what we are doing is all that really matters, then we ought not to be surprised if God leaves us to ourselves. We must come to the end of ourselves and begin, with God's help, to call upon him, as these Cornish Christians did with an urgency and an insistence which will not be denied. The Bible teaches us the absolute necessity of this. The whole history of the church reinforces the lesson.

Their view of the Spirit

In these years the Methodists gave much more prominence to the Holy Spirit than we do. This finds expression in Charles Wesley's hymns, and in their reports upon the work of God. They knew how dependent they were upon the working of the Spirit. Without the Holy Spirit there can be no faith, no joy and no hope. The reaction in many evangelical churches to the Charismatic Movement has been so extreme that there is almost a total neglect of the Holy Spirit in some circles; and in a number of evangelical churches he has become an embarrassment and is hardly ever mentioned. The greatest insult we can give anyone is to totally ignore him. If we are quenching the Spirit and grieving him in this way then it is not surprising that our prayers for revival are unheard.

Perhaps it is significant that most of the men whom God used in the revivals of the eighteenth and nineteenth centuries were not actually praying for revival when revival came. This is illustrated by the members of the Holy Club in Oxford and by the early Primitive Methodists. They were *seeking God* with a holy zeal; they desired to please God in every part of their lives; and they sought with much diligence the good of the souls of their fellow-men. This should cause us to rethink our view of revival, and to this we will turn in our next chapter.

8

RETHINKING OUR DOCTRINE OF REVIVAL

In 1959 Dr David Martyn Lloyd-Jones of Westminster Chapel, London, preached a series of sermons on the subject of revival to commemorate the centenary of the 1859-65 revival. These were followed up by a series in 1964-65 on the baptism of the Holy Spirit in which he argued that the whole character of the life of the church should be marked by outpourings of the Holy Spirit such as we observe in the history of the Christian church.

However, after the sixties he became aware of a somewhat distorted emphasis being placed on the subject of revival, giving rise to disillusionment and a negative reaction to the whole matter, and in the remaining years of his life he said far less about it,[1] though he did not change his basic position. He always regarded revival as the church's greatest need.

The concentration in the earlier chapters on notable revivals of religion should not lead us to depreciate the regular and ongoing life and work of the churches. A preoccupation with revival on a grand scale can so swamp our thinking that nothing else is regarded as being of any importance or significance. In addition we can arrive at a view of revival which is more mystical than biblical. After all, the word 'revival' is not used in the New Testament, and though it is a perfectly legitimate way of referring to the working of the Holy Spirit in great power, we need to be careful that we do not import into the term ideas and emphases for which there is no biblical justification. And we should be careful not to romanticize the subject so that we find ourselves adrift from biblical realities. The effect of extreme emphases has been to set some people totally against the subject of revivals — particularly in England. On the other hand, it has brought some who are concerned for revival to neglect necessary biblical duties and to minimize the more normal and usual operations of the Spirit of God. While aware of the dangers of a distorted view of revival, we believe that the greater danger lies in denial of the concept. Those who oppose the necessity of revivals frequently also neglect the person and work of the Holy Spirit in the experience of the believer and of the church. The Christian life then becomes formal and lacking in experimental religion.

We pray for 'revival'. *But what exactly do we mean by 'revival'?* There are those who would hardly consider some of the movements recorded in the earlier chapters of this book as actual revivals. Why their hesitation? The revivals do not fit their view of what a revival should be. Many took place in denominations that were Arminian in theology, and that is a problem for some. And in a number of revivals there was a degree of excitement which they do not find attractive. Then there are others reluctant to regard the spiritual awakening and growth in the Baptist and Congregational churches as revival. Where, they may ask, was all the deep feeling and emotion that is usually associated with revivals? The answer is that though it was less emphasized, it was by no means absent.

One factor that we need to bear in mind is the temperamental differences which exist between various peoples. The

Cornishman of the period we have considered was highly excitable by nature. It is to be expected that this aspect of personality would continue to express itself in times of revival — and may frequently predominate. But we must not insist on such exuberance as a necessary feature of revival. Likewise, the distinctive characteristics of the Scottish, the Welsh and the English are not to be regarded as either essential or as a liability in our evaluation of revival.

Bearing this in mind, if revival were to break out today, many of us who pray for it might fail to recognize it; indeed, we might openly oppose it on account of the rigidity of our doctrinal position, or by reason of ingrained prejudices or ultra-traditionalism. Judging from the readiness of some evangelicals in our own day to divide over such secondary issues as hymn books, versions of the Bible, and instruments used in worship, we question whether a spiritual awakening would be to the liking of many, even though they have prayed for revival. History reminds us that all sorts of unusual phenomena accompany revivals, and human traditions are often changed.

So it is necessary to ask again: What exactly do we mean by 'revival'? *Where do we find the doctrine in Scripture?* Is it legitimate to refer to the reformations and restorations of the nation of Israel in the Old Testament as revivals? The religious transformations brought about in the days of Elijah, Hezekiah, Josiah, Zerubbabel, Ezra and Nehemiah, each accompanied to different degrees by the suppression of idolatry and the forsaking of evil practices, were often more an expression of the godly zeal of the leaders than a change in the spiritual condition of the people. This was also true of the era of the Judges to some extent, though it has to be said that each period of restoration described in that book was preceded by a measure of repentance and a general calling upon the name of the Lord by the people. We often use the Psalms when speaking of revival, Psalms such as 44, 74, 79, 80, 85, 89 and 126, but are we entirely justified in doing this? The difference between Israel as a theocratic nation and the church as a spiritual people has to be borne in mind; yet it is surely right to identify times of repentance and of calling upon God for his intervention as providing us with spiritual principles as to what prevails with God in securing his favour and blessing upon his people.

Those who oppose any emphasis upon revival often point out that there is nothing in the New Testament to support it. Nowhere in the New Testament are we urged to pray for revival. The answer sometimes given to this objection is that the New Testament church was in the midst of revival and therefore had no need to pray for revival. This is an argument from silence, and not a very convincing one. Were the churches in Asia addressed in Revelation 1-3 in the midst of revival? Replicate them in the modern context and most would not be regarded as churches in a revived condition. Yet they were not exhorted to pray for revival — they were exhorted to repent. And is not this a more important note? Whether or not it leads to revival is in the hands of God.

So is our doctrine of revival a New Testament concept, or have we created, as some claim, a romanticized view for which there is little New Testament justification? This is an important question since at the present time there is considerable disillusionment with the whole concept of revival, even among some who once contended strongly for it. They maintain that the word *revival* is not found in the New Testament. But neither is the word *Trinity* and yet that doctrine is found on almost every page. A word does not have to occur in the New Testament for the doctrine it represents to have New Testament validity. Even so, we must surely be able to anchor our doctrine of revival in the New Testament and use New Testament terms to justify it. And this is even more necessary if we would deliver it from those emphases frequently associated with it which have tended to bring it into disrepute.

How then are we to define revival?

There is a danger of creating a revival stereotype. It demands certain detailed characteristics that are frequently more mystical than doctrinal, more dependent on emotions and feelings rather than truth. Those who have this view of revival would be uneasy with Merle d'Aubigne's description of the Reformation as a revival. We are also in danger of a very subjective evaluation of what is, and what is not revival, and sometimes this means that we judge whether a spiritual movement is revival by its conformity or otherwise to the characteristics of some past work of God which happens to appeal to us.

If our concept of revival cannot be doctrinally defined, then it is in danger of becoming an unbiblical mysticism. But this seems to be the view of some friends who think of revival as an indefinable 'it' or a highly charged spiritual ethos. And they read into this notion vague ideas of emotional, sentimental and even occultic phenomena. They think of revival as being quite different in its essence from the usual life and experience of the church, totally distinct from the normal operations of the Holy Spirit. This we believe to be wrong. In his *History of Wesleyan Methodism*[2] George Smith defines revival as follows:

> A revival, therefore, is a work of grace effected by the Spirit of God on the souls of men; and, in its nature, differs only from the ordinary operations of the Holy Ghost, in the enlightening and conversion of men, by its wider prevalence and greater intensity.

This quotation affirms that revival is not different in *essence* from any other true work of God, but only in *degree* of power and *extent* of the work.

We must ground our definition of revival in the regular New Testament teaching on the person and work of the Holy Spirit.

If we move away from this, we are liable to produce a concept that is not biblical; some are in danger of doing this.

If, as we would argue, *the characteristics of revival are no different from the characteristics of any normal working of the Holy Spirit except in terms of intensity and extent,* it follows that to describe as 'revival' any true work of the Holy Spirit in awakening the souls of men and in spiritually quickening the church is a somewhat relative and subjective judgement. If there were an occasion when the presence of God was strongly felt and five people were wonderfully converted, would that be revival? Or should it be twenty-five people or fifty? Who is to say?

So before turning to any of the problems arising from our doctrine of revival, we must ask a question.

What are the characteristics of a work of the Holy Spirit?

The Scriptures would suggest the following elements:

1. *The supernatural* — 'the finger of God' or the touch of heaven upon earth. Salvation is God's work. It cannot be accounted for in human terms. The church is God's special creation in and through Jesus Christ (Ephesians 2:10). And the true life of a church is that which results from a work of the risen Christ by the Holy Spirit. Man cannot produce it by his own efforts, nor can he work it up in any way. So we can say of revival, with Jonathan Edwards, that it comes down from heaven and is not worked up on earth.

2. *A consciousness of God.* A clear sense of his manifest presence, and of his holiness and glory. This happens in conversions and when God is blessing the churches, and it happens to a *marked degree* in revivals.

3. *Conviction of sin leading to repentance.* 'And when He has come, He will convict the world of sin, and of righteousness, and of judgement...' (John 16:8-11). People are never naturally convicted of their sin; by nature we are self-justifying. A specific work of the Spirit is required. And when the Spirit works, sin becomes abhorrent, leading a person to hate and forsake it (2 Corinthians 7:9-11). Much preaching today omits the doctrine of sin and repentance.

4. *A crying out to God for mercy through Jesus Christ.* We have lost this note in our churches. People are urged to make some commitment to Christ but are rarely exhorted to call upon God for mercy. One reason for this is that we no longer seem to believe in the wrath to come (Romans 1:18; 1 Thessalonians 1:10). But without it the gospel message makes little sense. So this calling upon God for mercy is an essential element of repentance (Luke 18:13-14).

5. *A glorifying of the person of the Lord Jesus Christ.* Jesus said of the Spirit, 'He will glorify Me, for He will take of what is Mine and declare it to you' (John 16:14).

6. *Joy in salvation and in God.* This is a strong feature in times of revival and yet is so often lacking amongst us.

7. *A spirit of prayer.* This is evidence of men and women humbled before their God and Maker.

8. *A sense of the eternal world* — so lacking from our earthbound age.

Much could be written on each of these features of the working of the Holy Spirit. They are characteristics of his activity whenever and wherever he works. We must therefore not put revival into a different category of the Holy Spirit's work, even though it may appear so to those caught up in a revival.

The point can be illustrated as follows. Here is a man who has lived without any real sense of God or of the seriousness his sins, and a day dawns when he becomes aware of God. He experiences deep conviction of sin and begins to seek God, often with a sense of desperation. He does this until he is brought to repentance and looks away to the Lord Jesus Christ for pardon and salvation. Then he is given an assurance of God's mercy and the forgiveness of his sins. And this is followed by great joy and gladness. We all know of cases like this, do we not? Just one person is touched. However, if this were to happen to one hundred people in the same locality within a short space of time, then we should speak of it as 'revival', and quite rightly so. But when it happens to only one person, we ought not to despise the 'day of small things', or to be despondent. It is of the essence of revival, even though we cannot call it revival. We could describe it as 'a touch of revival'.

The New Testament teaching on the Holy Spirit as it relates to revival

Before his ascension into heaven Jesus commanded his disciples to remain in Jerusalem and 'to wait for the Promise of the Father' (Acts 1:4). They were to 'be baptized with the Holy Spirit not many days from now' (v. 5). And Jesus added, 'But you shall receive power when the Holy Spirit has come upon you; and you shall be witnesses to Me in Jerusalem, and in all Judea and Samaria, and to the end of the earth' (v. 8). The fulfilment of this promise took place on the Day of Pentecost as described in Acts 2. How do we understand this event? Many would argue that this was when the New Testament church came into being as one body. But there is no reference to this in the account. Also, some maintain that at this time the disciples in Jerusalem first received the Holy Spirit, but in fact they were regenerated by the Holy Spirit before Pentecost (cf. Matthew 16:13-17). They had received his indwelling when Jesus had breathed on them following his resurrection and said, 'Receive the Holy Spirit' (John 20:22); nothing in this passage suggests that this was merely symbolic of what was to come, or that it was some sort of prophetic utterance.

Pentecost was the day when the disciples were 'endued with power from on high' as the Lord had promised (Luke 24:49). And it was this empowerment that enabled the early church to bear witness to Jesus Christ with such authority and influence. Pentecost introduced the New Covenant age in which the ascended Lord Jesus Christ continues his work on earth through the supply of his Spirit to his church. This is the substance of the Acts of the Apostles: a continuation of what Jesus had begun to do and teach whilst here on earth (Acts 1:1f.). Pentecost was a baptism of power by the Holy Spirit to equip the church for this task. It was not 'once for all' as though no further outpourings were required. Indeed, shortly after Pentecost, when the disciples had been threatened by the authorities they prayed for boldness and power to continue their witness, and we read 'the place ... was shaken; and they were all filled with the Holy Spirit' (Acts 4:31). They were endued and filled afresh with power from on high.

Surely, this is how the church has to operate: asking and receiving, praying and being empowered with fresh supplies of the Holy Spirit's energies. Such is the pattern of the book of Acts. We noted earlier, but it can bear repetition, that though Jesus received the Holy Spirit 'without measure' (John 3:34, ESV), or 'without limit' (NIV), his servants cannot be trusted in the same way. We must pray again and again for *fresh* supplies of the Holy Spirit, so ensuring that the church is kept in a humbled position before God (cf. Philippians 1:19). This means that we have to keep praying and asking. The early church did this, and so must we. The whole work of God depends upon it. The work is carried on and promoted by fresh unction from the Holy Spirit. Every preacher should know something about this. Sometimes he will preach with unusual spiritual power, but this does not mean that the next time he preaches he will have the same divine assistance. He has to keep seeking fresh supplies of the Spirit's power.

This is the model of the gospel age — the Pentecostal age — the age in which power flows to the church on earth from the ascended Christ in heaven to fulfil the purposes for which he suffered and died. So there are variations of the Spirit's power within the church. A single gathered church may be given a measure of the Spirit and the people be blessed by God week by week; but there are times of special quickening and the people know it; and then there are seasons of unusual power and blessing. When this takes place we may speak of *revival*. Each of these conditions is of the same essence, in that Christ comes to his people, the Holy Spirit is at work and the presence of God is felt.

But sometimes there is a loss of power, and a coldness and lifelessness pervades the church; it seems as though God is absent from his people. The church no longer enjoys spiritual life; though people frequently mistake a high degree of activity for life and may be deceived into a misleading complacency. How does such a blight come upon the church? The Holy Spirit is a person, and if he is taken for granted or ignored, then he is grieved. At other times he is quenched by the attitudes, actions and sins of the Lord's people. So before there can be a discernible work of the Holy Spirit in the church once more, there has to come a time of purging and repentance. But when God is again pleased to work, 'times of refreshing' come from the presence of the Lord (Acts 3:19). The church is not a deep freeze in which the blessings of Pentecost are kept in store for the people of God to draw upon at will. There has to be continued effusions and supplies of the Spirit throughout the history of the church, and when these are given in an unusual degree we call it revival.

Having grounded the doctrine of revival in the New Testament and noted the principles of spiritual life which apply to the church in this gospel age, we are now in a position to consider some of *the problems which have arisen from the doctrine of revival*, and to suggest some solutions.

Most of these problems arise from the fact that many have been praying for as long as fifty years for revival in the United Kingdom and there appears to be no answer to their prayers. The last significant revival was 1904/5, over one hundred years ago; so to keep praying with no obvious answer to our prayers can have a seriously discouraging effect. So the first problem is that of *discouragement*. How do we deal with it? One way adopted by some is to urge the discouraged person just to keep on praying and to point out that persistence and importunity are necessary ingredients in prayer. The parable of the persistent widow in Luke 18:1-8 is often quoted to reinforce this emphasis, 'that men always ought to pray and not lose heart' (v. 1). But though the exhortation and the parable is of importance for us all, we must not lose sight of the fact that the widow *was heard*. In an earlier parable of the friend who comes seeking bread at midnight, Jesus sought to enforce the principle of perseverance in prayer (Luke 11:5-8) and added, 'So I say to you, ask, and it will be given you; seek, and you will find; knock, and it will be opened to you. For everyone who asks receives, and he who seeks finds, and to him who knocks it will be opened' (vv. 9-10). Again we need to note the fact that the man seeking bread received it on account of his importunity; the point of the Lord's exhortation to perseverance in prayer is that such perseverance will be rewarded by a definite answer.

The problem that many of us face in having prayed so long for revival is that our prayers seem to have remained unanswered. To have these parables quoted as a suggested solution to our discouragement serves only to accentuate the problem. This discouragement has been very common amongst ministers, and in some cases has given rise to other problems, one of which is a widespread *disillusionment* with the whole concept of revival. Where such a reaction has been resisted, many have faced the problem of *depression,* leading in some cases to virtual *despair.* Many have felt that God has been deaf to their cries. This has resulted in another problem: *a loss of confidence in prayer.*

Now we know that sometimes God does not answer the prayers of his people in their lifetime, prayers such as the cry for the conversion of a son or a daughter. And yet they have been subsequently converted. But we also know that the problems we have mentioned need to have a viable solution, so that they are overcome. The issue before us is how that is to be achieved. One way to deal with these problems is to adjust to some extent our view of revival and the place it has in the work of God. Are we right to elevate the notion of revival with the suggestion that all else is of little or no account? To imply that revival is something unique and distinct in *essence* from the more normal working of the Spirit is to fall into this way of thinking. And this can lead not only to the problems already mentioned, but to another, namely that of *an attitude of passivity* where we are found waiting for God to do something unique and feel unable to do anything ourselves. A paralysis of passivity is God-dishonouring. God *is* pleased to answer many prayers, and we can pray for those measures of the Spirit we need in the present work of God — in preaching, in bearing witness, and in the various opportunities we have of serving God. The fact that God has not chosen in our day to send a general awakening in our land does not mean that he has failed to answer many prayers for divine assistance and power. We must learn to see God's answers to our prayers in the works of the Spirit which take place on a lesser scale, but which are of the same grace and the same essence found to a larger degree in revivals. We must not set what God does in revival over against what God does at other times. A conversion in normal times is just as supernatural and wonderful as a conversion in revival times. And is not the God of revivals the same God of faithfulness, power and grace with whom we deal at the present time?

There is another and even better way of dealing with the problems arising from our preoccupation with revival. What were the men of the Holy Club in Oxford from 1729 onwards seeking: the Wesleys, Whitefield, Benjamin Ingham and others? What were they praying for? It was not revival. As we have noted, they were thirsting after God and desiring holiness of life. There is something much more important than seeking revival. It is seeking the God of revivals. We need to know God more fully! Let us thirst after him! Let us seek a manifest presence of Jesus Christ! Let us seek holiness of life! Let us hunger and thirst after righteousness! Such holy pursuits are not to the exclusion of a desire and prayer for revival, but they are of even greater importance. And God will not disappoint those who long for him. 'And you will seek Me and find Me, when you search for Me with all your heart' (Jeremiah 29:13; cf. James 4:8; Deuteronomy 4:29). And you will not need to wait a lifetime!

Finally, we must bear in mind what God may be doing with us in withholding some of his greater blessings from the church. J. H. Bavinck expressed it movingly in the following words:

Sometimes we feel almost powerless. With fear and trembling we can only try each day anew to live close to God, and we can pray. More than ever before in our own weakness, we experience that God alone can help us and that he will help, if we pray. Thus, we learn in these tense years to understand again what Paul had learned by prayer and tears, namely, that the power of Jesus Christ is revealed to the fullest only in our weakness, and that therefore — no matter how contradictory it may appear — it is possible to take comfort in our own impotence.[3]

GLOSSARY OF TERMS

Arianism: named after Arius (c.250-c.336) who taught that Jesus was not eternal, but was created by God the Father, and became the Son of God by his own merit. The heresy denies the true divinity of Jesus Christ.

Arminianism: the system of doctrine taught by Arminius (1560-1609). Denies the Calvinistic doctrine of predestination, and affirms that man has free will, independent of God. Salvation is all of grace, but man has the power freely to accept or reject the gospel.

Calvinism: that interpretation of Scripture named after John Calvin (1509-64), who taught in common with most of the Reformers the authority of Scripture, particular election and redemption, the moral inability of man in sin, irresistible grace and the final perseverance of believers.

Clapham Sect: a loosely-knit body of influential evangelical Anglicans, most of whom lived near Clapham in the latter years of the eighteenth and early years of the nineteenth centuries. They supported many social and religious causes. The 'saints', as they were called, included William Wilberforce, Henry Thornton, John Venn (rector of Clapham parish from 1792-1813), Thomas Clarkson, Charles Grant, James Stephen, Zachary Macaulay, Granville Sharp and others. They sought by good works and political influence to bring about social change, and were behind the abolition of the slave trade (1807), the formation of the British and Foreign Bible Society (1804), the establishment of the model colony of Sierra Leone and many other schemes for the betterment of society.

Dissenters: a general term for those Nonconformists who dissented from the Church of England following the Elizabethan Settlement, and sought to establish non-episcopal churches of a biblical character. The term came into regular use after the Glorious Revolution of 1688 to describe Baptist, Congregational (or Independent) and Presbyterian congregations. They were little influenced by the eighteenth-century Evangelical Revival, and were later designated the Old Dissent to distinguish them from the churches which were formed from the revival and described as the New Dissent. In the nineteenth century all these Nonconformists were described simply as Dissenters.

Enlightenment: the movement of rationalistic thought which arose in Germany and France in the eighteenth century, and was opposed to all supernatural religion, and held to the all-sufficiency of human reason. Believed in the essential goodness of man and sought happiness in this life as its great ideal. Retained belief in God and in human freedom and immortality.

Eternal justification: The doctrine taught by Dr John Gill and his associates among the Particular Baptists and others influenced by him that the justification of the elect is from eternity and does not take place at the time the sinner believes in Jesus Christ. This reduces faith to a persuasion by the sinner that he has already been justified. No longer is the sinner urged to look to Christ to be justified by faith. Instead he has to seek the subjective conviction that he is one of the elect already justified through Jesus Christ.

High Calvinism: that form of Calvinism which held that the gospel should be preached to every creature, but considered it wrong to urge sinners indiscriminately to repent and believe in Jesus Christ. A direct application of the gospel should be reserved for 'sensible sinners', such as have been awakened by the Holy Spirit to the truth of the gospel.

Hyper-Calvinism: a more extreme and fatalistic form of Calvinism whose advocates did not believe in a general preaching of the gospel but held the view that God would save the elect when he chose to give them faith and repentance in his own time. They believed that the lost were under no obligation to repent and believe, since they had no ability to do this.

Oxford Movement: a movement (1833-45) within the Church of England which sought to restore the High Church doctrine and practice of the seventeenth century. They were opposed to the growing liberalism and worldliness within the church, and launched a series of *Tracts for the Times* designed to reaffirm apostolic succession and to propagate their sacramental views.

Pelagianism: a form of doctrine which denies original sin, and maintains the essential goodness of human nature. Teaches that man is capable of a life of holiness, and is able, therefore, to bring about his own salvation in response to divine exhortations and Christ's example.

Reformed: another term for the Calvinistic doctrine of the Reformers. Man is a fallen creature, enslaved in sin, and is totally dependent upon God for salvation. It is God's work to save sinners by his grace in Jesus Christ, and this grace is operative throughout salvation. By 'Reformed doctrine' is understood that interpretation of Scripture embodied in the *Thirty-Nine Articles of the Church of England*; the *Westminster Confession of Faith* (1647); the *Savoy Declaration of Faith* (1658); and the *Baptist Confession of Faith* (1677).

Semi-Pelagianism: denies original sin and affirms the essential goodness of human nature. But man needs the help of the Holy Spirit in the path of salvation. He has a freedom of will and a capacity for good works, but needs the co-operative grace of the Holy Spirit to obtain salvation.

Socinianism: a system of belief associated with the works of Socinus (1525-62). He questioned the doctrine of the Trinity, and rejected the full authority of Scripture. His approach to the Christian faith was rationalistic. Socinianism is expressed in Unitarian views.

Tractarian Movement: another term for the Oxford Movement. Arose from a series of *Tracts for our Times* (1833-41), written mainly by John Henry Newman, E. B. Pusey and John Keble and maintaining that the Church of England was not a department of State, but rather a branch of the holy, catholic and apostolic Church of Christ.

NOTES

Chapter 1

1. Richard Treffry Jr, *Memoirs of Rev. John Smith (1794-1831)*, 12th ed. 1881, p.151f.
2. Deuteronomy 32:7ff; Isaiah 46:9; 48:3.
3. For example, Psalms 44 & 126.
4. Jonathan Edwards, *Works*, Banner of Truth Trust, 1974, vol. i, p.539.
5. See chapter 8 for comments on the nature of a revival.
6. Harper Press, 2007, pp.8-12.
7. Owen Chadwick, *The Victorian Church*, Part I, A. & C. Black, 1971, p.400.
8. *A Short History of the English People*, Harper Edition, 1899, pp. 736f, quoted by Arnold Dallimore, *George Whitefield*, vol. i, Banner of Truth Trust, 1970, p.32.
9. *Portrait of an Age*, Oxford Paperbacks, OUP, 1960, p.4f.
10. *Ibid.*, p.5.
11. Quoted in J. Edwin Orr, *The Eager Feet, Evangelical Awakenings, 1790-1830*, Moody Press, 1975, p.183.
12. Richard F. Lovelace, *Dynamics of Spiritual Life: an Evangelical Theology of Renewal*, Paternoster, 1979, p.369ff.
13. *Life and Letters of Lord Macaulay*, 1908 edition, p.45.

Chapter 2

1. Michael Haykin, *One Heart and One Soul*, Evangelical Press, 1994, p.164. Chapter 8 of this book gives an excellent survey of the events connected with the 1784 Call to Prayer.
2. D. E. Jenkins, *The Rev. Thomas Charles of Bala*, vol. ii, 1908, p.89.
3. *Ibid.*
4. *Ibid.*, p.93f.
5. *Ibid.*, p.100.
6. *Ibid.*, p.98.
7. Samuel Dunn, *Memoirs of Mr Thomas Tatham and of Wesleyan Methodism in Nottingham*, London, 1847, p.148.
8. James Sigston, *Memoir of the Life and Ministry of William Bramwell*, 1820, p.163.
9. *Review* 33, July 1861, p.507.
10. See Deryck W. Lovegrove, *Established Church, Sectarian People: Itinerancy and the Transformation of English Dissent 1780-1830*, OUP, 1988.
11. John Walford, *Memoirs of the Life and Labours of Hugh Bourne*, ed. Rev. W. Antliff, vol. i, 1855, p.98.
12. See chapter 5 for full details.
13. Cp. similar effects of divine outpourings in Nottingham, see pp.35-6.
14. George Smith, *History of Wesleyan Methodism*, vol. iii, 1861, p.65.
15. Andrew Reed, *The Revival of Religion: A Narrative of the State of Religion at Wycliffe Chapel*, London: 1840, p.7.
16. *Ibid.*, p.8.
17. *Ibid.*, p.13.
18. *Ibid.*, p.17.
19. *Ibid.*, p.18.
20. Further and fuller accounts of Reed's life and ministry are found in *Memoirs of Andrew Reed*, edited by his sons, Andrew and Charles Reed, 1863; Ian J. Shaw, *High Calvinists in Action*, OUP, 2002, pp.279-322; Ian J. Shaw, *Andrew Reed: The Greatest is Charity*, Evangelical Press, 2005.
21. *Northern Baptist* magazine, 1839, p.23.
22. See chapter 4, pp.68-70.

Notes

Chapter 3

1. Henry W. Clark, *History of English Nonconformity*, 1913, vol. 2, p.314f.
2. J. R. & A. E. Gregory, *New History of Methodism*, vol. 1, p.413.
3. S. Pearce Carey, *Samuel Pearce: the Baptist Brainerd*, c. 1911, pp.183-4.
4. See chapter 5 of *History of the English Calvinistic Baptists, 1771-1892*, R. W. Oliver, Banner of Truth Trust, 2006.
5. Thomas Whitehead, *The History of the Dales Congregational Churches*, 1930, p.35.
6. *Op. cit.*, S. Pearce Carey, p.41f.
7. James Sigston, *Memoir of the Life and Ministry of William Bramwell*, 1820, p.65.
8. *Ibid.*, p.66.
9. *Ibid.*, p.67.
10. *Ibid.*, p.72.
11. *Ibid.*, p.76.
12. *Arminian Magazine*, December 1794.
13. *Ibid.*, pp.604-5.
14. *Ibid.*, pp.605-6.
15. *Ibid.*
16. *Ibid.*, p.651.
17. *Ibid.*, p.606f.

Chapter 4

1. *London Methodist Magazine*, XVIII, p.415f.
2. *Ibid.*
3. *Ibid.*
4. *Memoir of Bramwell*, *op.cit.*, p.104f.
5. *Ibid.*, p.190.
6. George Smith, *History of Methodism*, vol. ii, 2nd edition 1862, p.418ff.
7. See *Praying Johnny, or The Life and Labours of John Oxtoby*, Harvey Leigh, 1856; and *Life of John Oxtoby*, George Shaw, 1894, reprinted 2002.
8. Joseph Ritson, *The Romance of Primitive Methodism*, 1909, p.114.

9. H. B. Kendall, *The Origin and History of the Primitive Methodist Church*, vol. II, 1905, p.106.

10. *Op. cit.*, p.114 f.

11. George Smith, *History of Wesleyan Methodism*, vol. iii, p.48.

12. See p.63.

13. See Robert Young, *Showers of Blessing: Sketches of Revivals of Religion in the Wesleyan Methodist Connexion*, 1844, p.373ff; and *The Methodist Magazine*, 1834, p.446.

14. *Early Victorian Methodism — the Correspondence of Jabez Bunting, 1830-1858*, ed. W. R. Ward, OUP, 1976, p.84.

15. *Ibid.*, p.142.

16. *The Northern Baptists*, London, 1839, pp.224-226.

17. See earlier comments, pp.44-6.

18. *Op.cit.*, p.276.

19. *Ibid.*, p.210.

20. John Taylor, *Reminiscences of Isaac Marsden*, London, 1892, p.183.

21. *Ibid.*

Chapter 5

1. A. L. Rowse, *A Cornish childhood*, 1924; Martin Pugh, *We danced all night, a social history of Britain between the Wars*, The Bodley Head, 2008, pp.414-15.

2. G. E. Cell, *The Rediscovery of John Wesley*, 1935, p.412.

3. *Memoir of William Carvosso*, 1835, p.36.

4. *Ibid.*, p.38.

5. *Wesleyan Methodist Magazine*, 1824, p.217.

6. *Wesleyan Methodist Magazine*, 1827, p.2.

7. Thomas Shaw, *A History of Cornish Methodism*, D. Bradford Barton Ltd, 1967, p.26.

8. This consisted of: Wesleyan 20.5%; Bible Christian 6%; Wesleyan Methodist Association 3.1%; Primitive Methodists 2%; Methodist New Connexion 0.2%; Wesleyan Reformed 0.2%.

9. George Smith, *History of Wesleyan Methodism*, vol. ii, 1858, p.551f.

10. *A Memoir of Mr William Carvosso*, edited by his son, Benjamin Carvosso, London, 1835, p.54. For the Redruth revival, see also Dunn's *Memoirs of Tatham*, p.192ff; *The Methodist Magazine*, 1814, pp.397-400; George Smith, *History of Wesleyan Methodism*,

vol. ii, 1862, pp.551-9; Abel Stevens, *The History of Methodism*, 1861, pp.490 (ii) – 491 (ii).

11. Quoted in *Religion and Society in England, 1790-1850*, W. R. Ward, Batsford, 1972.
12. George Blencowe, *The Faithful Pastor — A Memoir of the Rev. Benjamin Carvosso*, 1857, p.205.
13. *Memoir,* p.137f.
14. *Ibid.*, p.140.
15. See chapter 2, pp.32-3, and James Sigston, *Memoir of the Life and Ministry of William Bramwell*, 1820, p.163.
16. *Memoir of William Carvosso*, p.153f.
17. This phrase was a fairly common expression in those days though it may appear somewhat quaint to us.
18. *Ibid.*, p.155.
19. See chapter 2, p.40.

Chapter 6

1. *A Memoir of Mr William Carvosso*, edited by his son, Benjamin Carvosso, London, 1835, p.189f.
2. Cited by Peter Isaacs in *A History of Evangelical Christianity in Cornwall*, 2000, p.115.
3. *A Memoir*, p.248.
4. *Ibid.*
5. *Ibid.*, p.249.
6. *Ibid.*
7. *Ibid.*, p.253f.
8. *Ibid.*, p.319.
9. A recent book on revivals in Scotland suggests that revivals are more frequent than commonly thought. See *Glory in the Glen: a History of Evangelical Revivals in Scotland, 1880-1940*; Christian Focus, 2009, Tom Lennie.
10. See chapter 5, pp.73, 75-6.
11. *A Memoir*, p.94.
12. *Ibid.*, p.258f.
13. *Ibid.*, p.260.
14. *Ibid.*, p.261.
15. See pp.87-88.
16. *Early Victorian Methodism: the Correspondence of Jabez Bunting, 1830-1858*, ed. W. R. Ward, OUP, 1976, p.12.

17. *Ibid.*, p.225.
18. *Ibid.*, p.239.

Chapter 7

1. Quoted in *A History of Cornish Methodism,* Thomas Shaw, D. Bradford Barton Ltd, 1967, p.120.
2. *Ibid.*, p.120.
3. *Systematic Theology,* vol. iii, 1880, p.484. The whole passage, pp.474-485, is helpful in this connection.
4. Roland Allen, *The Spontaneous Expansion of the Church,* World Dominion Press, 1960, p.9. It is to be regretted that this valuable book has been seriously neglected and never really answered, though it is of great relevance to missionary and evangelistic enterprise.
5. *Ibid.*, p.6.

Chapter 8

1. Perhaps it is significant that his sermons on revival did not appear in book form in his lifetime. They were published in 1986 by Marshall Pickering under the title, *Revival.* This was five years after his death.
2. Vol. ii, 1858, p.617.
3. J. H. Bavinck, *An Introduction to the Science of Missions,* Presbyterian & Reformed Publishing Co., Philadelphia, 1960, p.217.

SELECTED BIBLIOGRAPHY

Books have been written on the second evangelical awakening in America, but little of a comprehensive character exists on the revivals which took place in the period 1790-1840 in England and Wales except for *The Eager Feet, Evangelical Awakenings, 1790-1830,* Moody Press, 1975, by J. Edwin Orr.

A Memoir of William Carvosso, edited by his son Benjamin Carvosso, 1835, deals fairly comprehensively with the Cornish revivals of that period associated with Wesleyan Methodism, and has been used to provide the outline for the material in chapters 5 & 6.

Showers of Blessings: Sketches of Revivals of Religion in the Wesleyan Methodist Connexion, Robert Young, 1844, is a valuable collection of letters, reports and information gathered from magazines, reviews, journals and biographies available to the author at that time. Much of his information is culled from *The Methodist Magazine,* annual copies of which are found in the Evangelical Library where the diligent reader will discover rewarding accounts of many revivals.

The Evangelical Magazine provides interesting material relating to both Baptist and Congregational churches of Calvinistic convictions. The Particular Baptists went their own way in 1813 with the *Baptist Magazine* first published in 1809. Volume 4 of the *History of the English*

Baptists, Joseph Ivimey, 1830 (in four volumes), is a hotchpotch of intriguing material. Henry W. Clark in volume II of his *History of English Nonconformity,* 1913, 2 vols, has some very perceptive observations.

Biographies are a fruitful source of material and much can be derived from such as:

The Memoir of the Life and Ministry of William Bramwell, James Sigston, 1820; *The Memoirs of the Life and Labours of Hugh Bourne,* John Walford, 1855 (two volumes bound in one) — a superb account of the early Primitive Methodists; *Autobiography of Rev. James Smith of Cheltenham,* 1862. All these contain fascinating and spiritually edifying accounts of the wonderful works of God.

The Lives of Robert and James Haldane, 1852, is an important work as it related to the revivals in Scotland and on the Continent. *Narrative of Revivals of Religion in Scotland, Ireland and Wales, 1839,* despite its title applies mainly to the Scottish revivals. *Glory in the Glen: a History of Evangelical Revivals in Scotland, 1880-1940,* Christian Focus, 2009, Tom Lennie, is also significant.

The Life of Thomas Charles of Bala, D. E. Jenkins, 3 vols., 1908, gives a thrilling account of the revivals in Wales. Volume 2 of *History of Methodism in Ireland,* G. H. Crookshank, 1886, 3 vols., describes vividly the amazing works of God in the years 1789-1820.

There are many scholarly standard and modern works on Nonconformity and Church History dealing with the early nineteenth-century from which valuable information and comments may be gleaned. Mention should be made of:

High Calvinists in Action (OUP, 2002), Ian J. Shaw; *Early Correspondence of Jabez Bunting, 1820-1829,* ed. W. R. Ward, Royal Historical Society, 1972; *Early Victorian Methodism: the Correspondence of Jabez Bunting, 1830-1858,* ed. W. R. Ward, OUP. 1976.

A History of the Evangelical Party, G. R. Balleine, 1909; *The Early Evangelicals,* L. E. Elliott-Binns, 1953; and *The Parting of Friends,* David Newsome, 1993, describe the strengths and expose the growing weaknesses of the Evangelicals within the Church of England over the period.

INDEX

Index

Enlightenment, 30, 126
Erskine, John, 32
eternal justification, 28, 126-7
Europe, 20-1, 27, 33
Evangelical Alliance, 27
Evangelical Awakenings, 18, 27
Evangelical Magazine, The, 19, 37
Evangelical Revival, 9, 10, 16-7, 18, 21, 22, 26, 29, 30, 50, 51, 52, 76, 93, 126
  decline of, 19-21, 30
evangelicalism, 10, 24, 27, 86
evangelicals, 10, 24, 47, 103
evangelism, 18, 28, 85, 93-4, 106, 108-10
Ezra, 71, 114

Falmouth, 87, 91
fellowship, 17
Filey, 64
Finney, Charles, 45, 65, 68-9, 108
Flieder, Theodore, 24-5
Flushing, 91-3
French Revolution, 30
Fry, Elizabeth, 24
Fuller, Andrew, 32, 69

Gadsby, William, 19
Geneva, 27, 40
Gill, John, 22, 126
God, 40, 50, 75, 82
  acts of, 14, 71, 101, 104
  blessing of, 46, 55, 85, 108, 117
  consciousness of, 117
  dependence on, 44, 45, 70, 104
  glory of, 13, 36, 83, 84
  grace of, 49, 51, 81, 83
  kingdom of, 17, 53
  love of, 61

mercy of, 23, 55, 104, 119
movement of, 78
power of, 15, 32, 46, 49, 55, 57, 58, 60, 61, 68, 78, 84, 85, 86, 94, 105
presence of, 46, 49, 60, 66, 97, 121
purposes of, 32
sovereignty of, 84, 85, 86, 97, 102, 106, 108
Word of, 47, 107
work(s) of, 20-1, 23, 28, 29-30, 36, 38, 41, 43, 45-6, 48, 53, 54-5, 57, 61-2, 63, 66, 67, 69, 80, 82, 85-6, 88, 92, 93, 97-8, 101-11
gospel, 17, 23, 50
  influence of, 26
  preaching of, 17, 46-7, 49, 69, 94, 102
  spread of, 16, 21, 26, 28, 29, 53, 85, 110
Great Awakening, 21
Great Commission, 108, 109
'Great Ejection' (1662), 51-2
Great Revival, The — see Redruth, 'The Great Revival'
Green, J. R., 23
Grimshaw, William, 16, 52-3
Guiseley, 66
Gwennap, 78
Gwennap Pit, 73, 74

Hague, William, 20
Haldane, James, 40
Haldane, Robert, 27, 40
Halifax, 60, 62
Hall, Robert, Sr, 32
Hanson, Thomas, 73-5
Harris, Howel, 16

Index